Stop Whining and Start Working

JUDY GAMAN

STOP
WHINING

—AND—

START
WORKING

A GUIDE TO **GETTING HIRED**

Stop Whining and Start Working: A Guide to Getting Hired

©2024 Judy Gaman

Gallup® and CliftonStrengths® are trademarks of Gallup, Inc. These trademarks are used with permission, all rights reserved. For more information about Gallup® and CliftonStrengths®, please visit https://www.gallup.com/home.aspx.

Paperback ISBN: 978-1-7363342-8-7

Ebook ISBN: 978-1-7363342-7-0

64 Squares

CONTENTS

"STRIVING FOR SUCCESS WITHOUT HARD WORK IS LIKE TRYING TO HARVEST WHERE YOU HAVEN'T PLANTED."

—David Bly, former senior copy editor at the *Calgary Herald*, author, photographer, and teacher

INTRODUCTION:
WHAT YOU HAVE TO GAIN

Since you're reading this book, there's a good chance you're looking to land a job. It could be your first job or a new job in the same field, or you might want to make a complete career change. Why should you read this book and commit to the exercises herein? You certainly have nothing to lose, and you have oh so much to gain, starting with taking control of your future. This book is designed to put you in the driver's seat of your career path. No more hoping, wishing, and wondering. Action—or a string of the right actions—is the only way to get the desired reaction.

I've written this book for those struggling with landing the right position and those hoping to land any position at all. Regardless of where you are on your employment journey, this book is designed to elevate your chances of turning an interview into a bona fide offer—an offer that will change the trajectory of your future. The book starts with the basics, gets deeper in thought, and gets tougher in the exercises as you go through them. Reading it front to back will be the most helpful—even if some of it is a review—because each chapter has a nugget of wisdom that may have you looking at your life a little differently. But if you're the kind of person who skips around, reading chapters out of order, that's okay, too. The content is evergreen, so it will be helpful today, tomorrow, and years from now should you find yourself looking for a job again.

By design, this book will ask you to take a good, hard look at your employability. The process will require you to remove the blinders, leave the victim mentality behind, and do some hard work on your own behalf. You must become your own cheerleader, manager of your reputation, and boss of your emotions. This isn't the type of book you pick up, read, set down, and "Poof!" your whole world has changed instantly. Instead, I'll ask you to see yourself the way a potential employer would see you. For many, this may be uncomfortable or unsettling because you'll be confronted with your past decisions, your current attitude, and all the ways you need to improve before moving forward. The good news is that this process is not disheartening; it's empowering.

Consider these chapters as tools in your toolbox. Your employability is in the shop, and you need to fix it. The repair may take some time to complete, but the idea is to fix your issues once and for all, leaving you with a bright, new image that will get employers to notice you. When used correctly over time, these tools will also help you climb the ladder of success for years to come as you excel in your field or discover new horizons.

Through this multistage process, you'll be able to unlock the reasons behind your past failures with job searches, unfruitful interviews, and positions that were not the right fit. You'll also learn what it takes to get the interview, nail that interview, and keep the job.

Long gone are the days that one sheet of paper will get you noticed. That's why this book will help you brand yourself as the perfect candidate for the jobs you seek. Keep in mind that the work doesn't stop there. Once you land a position, it's up to you to keep that position. Most of us never learned what's taught in these chapters in high school or college or from parents who sat their teens or adult children down to explain the process (not that many teens listen to their parents, anyway).

If you're ready to shoot straight with yourself and take control of your future, congratulations—you're in the right place. This is the first step in solving your unemployment, underemployment, or career-change woes. By the end of this book, you'll have worked diligently through the process and have what it takes to become desirable, memorable, and employable.

Perhaps the toughest chapter in the book comes at the end, where I ask you to discover your WHY and be true to it. This exercise will help you live in your purpose and your passion. The overarching goal of this book is first to help you obtain employment, but that's only part of a much greater purpose. By the end of this book, you will know what it takes to become a leader and secure a better future. You'll also uncover your WHY, the core desires behind the kind of future that will leave you feeling fulfilled and knowing you are in the right place. Now, let's get busy!

"YOUR FEARS WILL GROW SMALLER AND SMALLER AS YOU RISE ABOVE THEM."

—Carol "CC" Miller, founder of Positive Focus

CHAPTER 1

GETTING PAST DISCOURAGEMENT

Nobody hires an Eeyore. Remember him? He was made famous by A. A. Milne, the author who wrote the Winnie-the-Pooh series. Milne wanted to create a character who was depressed, pessimistic, and completely down on himself and his luck in every word he spoke. It was no accident that Eeyore was dark gray and a donkey. Gray is the color of doom and gloom, and everyone knows that a donkey is stubborn by nature. An Eeyore is someone who runs on low energy and brings down the energy of everyone around him, too. Don't be an Eeyore.

Unlike this fictional character who was subject to the whims of Milne, you are the cocreator of your life's story. You have the power to write your future of perseverance, hard work, and success. You also have the power to do the opposite. Either way, it's your decision. Outcome is the result of productive work you're willing to put in—or the lack thereof. You can't control the bad breaks you may have been dealt or will be dealt, but you can control how you handle such disappointments and whether you rise above them to find higher ground, better opportunities, and a clearer path.

Even if you lost your past job, your spouse left you, your best friend ghosted you, your dog died, and you felt all alone in the world, your life and your story would not be over; they are simply at a point of a new beginning. Turn that anger and frustration into fuel—rocket fuel that will propel you into a new dimension of your life. This is the point in time where you refuse to wear the weight of the victim's cloak and instead trade it in for your superhero cape.

You may be saying, "But you don't know me and what I've been through" or "I really screwed up my last job" or "I don't have the confidence to do this." Your inner dialogue may even say something as self-limiting as, "It's not me; it's everyone else." Language such as this is destructive and self-sabotaging. This sort of internal messaging must be turned off once and for all. How do you turn them off? Start with the exercise below.

Take a moment to write down all your negative internal messaging. Handwrite those thoughts onto paper so you can see them. Read them aloud and imagine hearing a friend say those things about themselves. How would you counsel that friend? If you're a good friend, you'd encourage them to overcome their past while also being honest about how their victim mentality is holding them back. Words, both spoken and in thought, have power. Hearing the words you're thinking will help you better understand the impact they may be making on your life. It's time to take control of your thought patterns.

Now that you've purged yourself of all these toxic thoughts by taking them from your head and heart and placing them on a page, they become tangible. You can now hold them in your hand and control their future. Put those words through a shredder, toss them into a fireplace, or find your unique way of saying goodbye to them. Make it formal. Have a funeral for them. Do whatever feels right for you. Don't just think about them and mentally bury them, because burying negative emotions without facing them amplifies the issues for a later date. It also allows time for them to gain more energy and exude more power over you.

The goal of this exercise is to destroy the negative words and phrases physically to take away their power. If you're a person of faith, pray for them to no longer plague you. Ask friends to hold you accountable should you fall into old habits and verbalize these toxic phrases ever again. Don't be afraid to ask others for help. Having an accountability partner can help you stay on track. Friends and family are always willing to help with these sorts of things. They're probably ready to hear you speak more positively, and they will welcome the change.

Once you've completed this exercise, you can continue reading. If you haven't completed the exercise yet, give yourself the time to do so. It's powerful, impactful, and a catalyst for you to move forward.

Importance of Affirmations

The mind is an interesting place, and it feels void and loss when things are taken away. Because of this, your mind will need something to fill itself back up. This is where affirmations come into play. Maybe you've heard of affirmations before, or you know people who write a few positive words to themselves and tape them onto their mirror, add them to their daily calendar, or recite them every day or several times a day. Why do people do this? Because they understand on some level that they can either let their mind wander back into old habits and negative territory, or they can create new habits and a positive mental environment moving forward.

Using helpful and goal-oriented affirmations is a great way to straighten that superhero cape every day. They point your thoughts in the direction you want to go to accomplish the things you want to accomplish. Affirmations are fluid, and they will change as your life goals change. They're forward-thinking visions of who you want to be. They should be specific, but just as important, they should be specific to you.

Many counselors, career or life coaches, and well-meaning people will advise you to think of three or four things you want to change about your life and write them down. Why? Because they know the importance of this technique. They know that writing things down, just like we did earlier, will give those things meaning and make them real enough to initiate some action. I remember my first 3-by-5-inch card of affirmations. It had these statements:

1. I am a person who makes my bed every morning.
2. I am someone who helps others.
3. I am dedicated to family dinner time.

This list came at a time when work had become overwhelming. I was on autopilot and felt I was losing a sense of myself as my hours were controlled by an ever-growing calendar of appointments, only to be constantly interrupted by checking my emails and social media accounts. Once I wrote these affirmations proudly in permanent marker on my white card, I taped that card to my bathroom mirror. Then, I read each one aloud after I brushed my teeth. These words were the first thing I spoke in the morning and the last I spoke before going to bed. Within weeks, I started making my bed without thinking about it. Within a month, I was sitting on the board of a battered women's shelter. After about six weeks, I was back in the kitchen, cooking with the kids and focusing on great dinner table conversation again.

Because I stayed focused on what was ahead of me, rather than being weighed down by my current circumstances, I was able to make changes in my life almost effortlessly. You can, too.

Do you remember when you learned to drive? Almost all new drivers struggle at first because their focus is on what they don't want to do. They don't want to hit the curb. They don't want to cross the line. And they certainly don't want to wreck the car. Their eyes dart from side to side as they try to stay in their lane and just get though the terrifying experience. Then after some time, even the most reluctant drivers take their focus off the periphery and look up and look forward.

Driving our life, much like driving a car, is about looking and moving forward. The more energy we spend looking from side to side, focused on the things that are wrong in our life, or the curbs we don't want to hit, the less energy we spend pressing forward toward our future. Some people are stuck in the driver's ed of life, afraid to get on the highway and take charge of where they're going. If that's you, it's time to graduate. Put your focus on the things you want to accomplish instead of the obstacles you don't want to encounter.

My early affirmations were achieved by doing simple actions. Make my bed—check. Cook dinner—check. Then, as I progressed in my personal discipline, I was able to set greater goals. Metaphorically, I was ready to get off the side streets and drive on the interstate. It was time to go further, to venture out, to explore who I could be and what I could accomplish.

It should be no surprise that the bigger the goal, the more steps it takes to accomplish it. Complex affirmations take more work, more discipline, and a more pronounced reason to tackle them. For example, one complex affirmation I had was: "I am an accomplished author." A goal like that meant I needed to dedicate an enormous amount of time to writing, do extensive research, learn new things, and take risks. I had to start by convincing myself I was up for the task. I didn't do this by telling myself all the things that could go wrong or listening to the naysayers. I did this by affirming with myself, by repeating my affirmation, and by acting on those affirmations. Now, I have seven books, many of which are award-winning. Without affirmations and dedication to those affirmations, I'd have zero.

My goal to become an accomplished author is much like your goal to advance your employability. Both goals are complex, take research, require you learn new things, and ask you to take a few risks. So let's start with simple goals that will strengthen your affirmation muscles and give you some step-by-step wins. Once you accomplish these, you can later move on to bigger and harder goals.

Take out a 3-by-5-inch card and think of three to four statements that will point you toward your future. While there are hundreds of possibilities, here are a few examples to get you started:

1. I am someone who practices interviewing.
2. I am someone who researches three jobs a day.
3. I take the time to research potential employers before applying.
4. I am learning new things about myself every day.
5. I am taking the time to work on my résumé.
6. I am a positive person, as evidenced by my thoughts and deeds for the day.
7. I am working through the process each day.
8. I am someone who cares about my online reputation.

Now that you have your 3-by-5-inch card, decide where to keep it. Remember, you need to look at it and read the words on it at least twice a day. Once you've mastered something on the simple affirmation list, replace it with a new simple affirmation until you have confidently completed at least six. This can take anywhere from a week to a month, depending on how dedicated you are to the process.

When you've mastered six simple affirmations, you'll be ready to tackle more complex affirmations. The complex ones will take more time and effort on your part and will sound more like the examples below:

1. I am landing a new job.
2. I am creating a new career path for myself.
3. My employability score is improving daily.
4. I am mastering the interview process.
5. I am someone who has excellent community involvement.
6. My career choices are expanding.
7. I am increasing my knowledge base daily.
8. I am improving my health, both mentally and physically.

This book will give you the tools you need to work through these types of goals.

Getting past discouragement requires action on your part. The more action you do, the more positive energy you create. It's that positive energy that will fuel your success. Every day, think of at least one action for each that will prove your affirmations are moving in the right direction. After you do one, do another. The more you do, the better you'll get at it.

As you make complex affirmations, you'll need to create a plan of attack. That means recognizing that each complex affirmation or goal will take several specific milestones. Each milestone consists of action steps you'll need to take. Steps that are written down, specific, and given a time frame are more likely to be accomplished. Accomplished steps equal accomplished milestones, which then equal accomplished goals. As you work through this book, there'll be many milestones toward the ultimate goal of landing your dream job. Celebrate your small successes as you move forward—and keep the end goal top of mind. Even the most monumental dreams can be realized by dividing and conquering each step in the process. A wise person once told me, "Nothing is hard. Some things just take longer and require more work. Those are the things worth doing."

Building Your Vision Board

If you're a visual person like I am, take some time to build a visual reminder of what you want your life to be like. Your career goals should be on there, but a vision board should also include other things like dreams, relationship goals, maybe the house you want to buy, or the degree you want to earn. While affirmations are designed to get you to take small actions, a vision board is tailored to the big picture and ultimate goals of your life. There is no right or wrong way to compile your board. Some vision boards are chaotic, with words and photos going every which way, while others may be organized and color-coded, block-designed, or graphed-out symmetrically. Why is that? Because people are different. We think differently, organize our thoughts differently, and certainly have our own forms of expression; therefore, the execution of board design is irrelevant. It just needs to speak to you and to your big-picture goals in your own language.

Here are the supplies you'll need for a vision board:

1. A poster board, foam board, cork board, or similar for the backdrop
2. Magazine or newspaper clippings, stickers from the craft store, printed photos or words from the internet, your own drawings, and other visual representations of your goals and dreams
3. Markers, string, colored paper, or anything else you want to use to enhance your board
4. Number and letter stickers
5. Glue or tape

Dream big and remember that big goals don't materialize instantaneously, which is why you need these reminders to help keep you on track. Once you have completed your vision board, hang it in a prominent place. Mine is in my bathroom, but I know plenty of people who hang theirs in their office, the kitchen, or by their bed. There's no wrong place to display it, just as long as it's visible to you. If you choose to share it with others you can, but that's not the purpose. Rather than a show-and-tell, this board is primarily for your eyes. It's a reminder of why you're working hard on your affirmations, of better days ahead, and that hard work leads to good things. Now for the hard work.

"IF YOU DON'T KNOW WHERE YOU'RE GOING, ANY ROAD WILL GET YOU THERE."

—Lewis Carroll, logician, mathematician, photographer, and novelist

CHAPTER 2

WHAT'S THE RIGHT JOB FOR ME?

We all have favorites—that's what makes us unique. Even when we were in school, we had subjects that we loved and others that we dreaded. If we didn't have individual tastes, Baskin-Robbins wouldn't have thirty-one flavors, stores would carry one style of clothing, the cereal aisle would be a single shelf, and there would be one channel on television. The same is true for our work style and professional preferences. When we find work that suits our style, going to work can be something to look forward to, rather than a nagging task to be completed. Anyone can get a J-O-B, but those who strategically approach the job search and who are keen on their own individual preferences are the ones who land in the right place. That's why it's important to be strategic while appreciating your individual likes and dislikes.

Many times, I've spoken to college students about finding their passion. Regardless of the school's size or whether it's rural or urban, most of the students have one thing in common: They limit their dreams. Not by what they don't know, but by what they do know. That's right—what they *do* know is what holds them back. I hear things like, "I'll probably go into dentistry because that's what my dad did," or "My mom and two of my aunts are nurses, so I thought I'd be a nurse." It's in our nature to default to our comfort zone and search for familiar ground. So many people unknowingly trade life-changing opportunities in exchange for familiarity.

The same rule of reference is true when we search for jobs. We often limit our search to job titles we know and industries to which we have some connection. Job sites like Indeed, Monster, and ZipRecruiter all know this. That's why they have employers categorize their job postings. It's all about holes and pegs. If your peg (résumé) fits the hole (job category), you may find a match during your search, or a potential employer may be matched to your résumé. This is a good start, but by no means does it uncover all the possibilities. A good example of this is the nurse who typed "RN position" and got a slew of hospital positions. This nurse had a passion for helping others, but the twelve-hour shifts and holiday hours kept her away from her family. Eventually, she gave in and begrudgingly accepted another position at a hospital closer to home because that's what she knew, and that's what showed up in her job search.

Take that same nurse—we'll call her Nancy—who decided she'd look for positions that didn't require an RN degree. Nancy still wanted to help people, so she searched "nonprofit" and the word "clinical." To her surprise, she found a medical nonprofit that was looking for a director of clinical services. While they listed many of her other talents—like leadership and strong computer skills—it was the fact that she had a degree as a registered nurse that afforded her the position. Nancy finally found the perfect position where she could use her skills, be paid well, and have enough free time to make her son's football games.

Then there is the architect who preferred to travel rather than stay behind a desk and found a fit designing communities in remote villages. Many people who have successful podcasts just repackaged their gift of gab. I even know a few accidental CEOs, people who honed skills while having many other titles until they knew enough to be the chief executive officer of an entire company.

My point is that it's okay to study a field of familiarity; just don't box yourself in with your limited knowledge of job opportunities in that field. Think outside the box of familiarity and consider all the possibilities. Look at all your skills, not just those that directly apply to your degree or work experience, and think of new ways to apply them. That's what Steve Jobs, Bill Gates, Jeff Bezos, and others did. Elon Musk has degrees in economics and physics. Whether you're a fan or not, I think it could be successfully argued that Elon is using both of those, just in a nontraditional sense.

I'm not saying we all need to be titans; I'm simply using these examples to inspire you to see the other side of the spectrum and to realize there's so much room between where you are and where your future could take you. Nobody handed these individuals their futures; they created them. You can and will create your future, too.

Identifying Your Comfort Zone

Draw a vertical line down the middle of a blank page. At the top and to the left of that line, write the words "Professions/ Jobs." At the top and to the right of that line, write the words "Affiliation/Familiarity." As you make your list on the left, leave a few blank spaces below each listing. This will give you room to make longer notes about that profession on the right. For example, you may write "Banker" on the left side and on the right, you may write things like "Dad's profession" or "My economics degree." Keep this list going so you can see where your influences are coming from. Even if you have no intention of going into the professions you list on the left, it's still worth listing and going through the exercise.

Continue making the list until you've run out of the jobs or professions you have some sort of connection with. Once you've finished the list, number them sequentially on the far left from "Most Interested" to "Least Interested," or from "Yes!" to "No Way." So if you have fourteen professions or jobs listed, start with the number one and label them through the number fourteen. Don't worry; this isn't a commitment to do what you put at the top of your list. It's just an exercise to help you understand your current and past prejudices toward or against certain jobs. If you want to take the exercise to the next level, then on the very far right list the reasons you like or hate the options you feel emotional about.

Let's take Scott, a person who grew up around the restaurant business, and see how this exposure impacted him. From a young age, he learned everything there was to learn—from cooking to busing tables. He may understand the restaurant business thoroughly and may even have pursued a business degree in hopes of someday taking over the family business. But when faced with the commitment of owning the family restaurant, Scott couldn't think of anything worse. Why? Because he watched his family work long hours, skip vacations, and have little time for family life. Now he's married with a child on the way, and like others who may be reading this book, he hopes to transition into a career that fits his current needs.

Finding the right job doesn't always mean that it's found down the path of least resistance. Likewise, the right job isn't necessarily the job that comes the easiest or pays the most. As for that job you thought you always wanted to do, maybe it doesn't pay what you need to live on. It isn't necessarily about finding the job you know the most about, nor is it the job that everyone else wants you to have. Even what appears to be the right job may turn out to be in the wrong location. As you search for the job that is the best fit for you, keep in mind that the right job, at the right time, in the right place isn't always obvious. It takes time and work, but when you find it, you'll be glad you went these extra steps.

Yes, you read that last paragraph right: the right job isn't necessarily the one that pays you the most. Why not? Because taking a job for the pay and then leaving that job three or six months later because you couldn't stand the people, you were underqualified, you compromised your morals, or any other reason will cost you more than you make in the long run. Future employers will want to know why you didn't stay, why you couldn't give a reference for that position, or why you gave up so quickly. Even more importantly, employers can sniff out opportunists a mile away. They may not hire you for fear you'll always be looking to chase the best deal.

Perhaps the most recent and notable opportunity curse has been with the medical community. Some traveling nurses went from hospital to hospital, state to state, often being paid more than physicians, during the pandemic, taking advantage of a supply-and-demand issue. Afterward, as hospitals looked to normalize their staffing, they were reluctant to hire nurses who worked at three, five, or even ten places over a three-year period. Often, they were put off by an applicant who was expecting to be paid eighty to a hundred dollars per hour simply because they got used to the lifestyle the unnaturally elevated salary afforded them. From the nurse's standpoint, returning to their regular salary was just as psychologically challenging.

Whatever the reason, taking the wrong job for the wrong reason can negatively influence your family, friendships, social life, and self-esteem. If you're like most humans on this planet, you won't be able to hide the frustration of being in a position that's not a fit. I'm not saying that unique opportunities are bad. It's essential to succeed and obtain new skills, better pay, and expanded opportunities; just do it in an environment that fosters growth while not hurting your future employability.

The mirror image of taking a high-paying job for the wrong reason is devoting all your time and resources to something you love that won't support you financially. This is where many people unfortunately get into trouble. They confuse a hobby with a profession. If you want to make your hobby, such as art, streaming, or being an influencer of some sort, your profession, it must start as a side gig. Hobbies and side gigs should never replace a real job until they meet the requirements of a real job, which includes a large enough net profit to support you and your family's needs financially.

I'm all about side gigs. They allow you to try something new without the risk of going all in. When done right, some side gigs can turn into wonderful careers that pay very well. The real key here is to understand the side gig's place until it's earned a promotion to a real job. A great book on this topic is *What If It Does Work Out? How a Side Hustle Can Change Your Life* by Susie Moore. This book is a great resource because Susie knows this topic well, and she's very clear on the "Don't quit your day job just yet" theme. Not only have I read this one a few times, I've given copies out to relatives and a number of people I mentor.

If you're thinking, "I can't possibly do a side gig and my job at the same time," I want you to consider how many hours in a week you may really have to devote to growing that gig into something bigger. Most people work forty to fifty hours a week, sleep roughly eight hours a night, and spend the rest of that time unproductive. Let that sink in for a moment. Even at fifty hours of work a week, there are still sixty-two nonsleeping, nonwork hours. I strongly suggest you record in a diary an hour-by-hour timeline of how you spend your days for two weeks. That's the best way to see where you're wasting time. For the record, let me clarify what counts as wasting time. Certainly, time spent with your significant other, your kids, and your parents is quality time. Surfing the internet, watching multiple videos on YouTube, binge-watching television shows, or scrolling through your social media feeds is the quintessential definition of wasted time.

Tip: Most smartphones come with the ability to track your screen time. Turn that feature on to get a clearer picture of your habits. The power of observation alone will help you become more conscious of what's robbing your time.

Warning: This exercise may be a bit depressing, especially when you consider that thousands of hours are wasted each year. The good news is that you now have data to drive your change. You can't fix what you don't know. Now that you know it, fix it.

Consider the Costs Associated with the Job

There is so much to consider when taking a job. Every job comes with a cost. Your duty is to weigh that cost against the gain. A net neutral is good, but a net gain is best. The easiest and best way to get to your net gain is to consider your time commitment, the pay you'll receive, and the emotional and physical toll the position and the commute will take on you.

As the CEO of a luxury medical practice, I have met many high-profile athletes. While the world may think these athletes hit the lottery, many have told us they may not have chosen that path if they had fully understood the toll it would eventually take on their bodies. While they dedicate only a fraction of their life to professional sports, there is often a sacrifice to their health, their marriage, and their mental well-being. It may also surprise you to learn that many retired athletes also suffer financially. This is primarily due to poor planning and lack of money management skills. What does this have to do with you? The lesson is that fame and good fortune aren't necessarily sustainable and can often come at a high cost. For some, that cost is worth it; for others, it's not. Just like these athletes, you need to weigh the costs of your own career choices as you plan your future. Don't just fall in love with the title.

Confucius says, "Choose a job you love, and you'll never have to work a day in your life." I prefer to modify that advice to say, "Choose a job you love that will also love you back. You'll never work a day in your life, and you'll live long and die happy."

My addition to that quote may be a bit misleading, as it's not necessarily up to a job to actively love you back or improve your longevity. It's more about choosing wisely so you feel the love of what you're doing more intensely than the sacrifice you'll ultimately make. Good choices come when you know your own taste. Identify your favorite flavor of life, and then stay dedicated to choosing it repeatedly.

As you learn and grow through this process, be open to the idea that your strengths may not lie where you thought they did. You may identify strengths that you didn't know you had. For this very reason, it's up to you to do homework on yourself before doing homework on any future employers.

The first course you need to take is the course on you. Learning more about what makes you tick will help you determine the kind of work that will metaphorically love you back because it gives you the freedom to focus on the things that are most important to you. When you're naturally interested, you'll naturally be a better employee, which helps you in the interview process. Because you understand your strengths, it will give you real talking points as you sell yourself to future employers. Likewise, identifying the areas that you don't excel in or have an interest in may keep you from accepting the wrong position.

When interviewing, be careful never to fall into the trap of "I like everything" or, my personal favorite, "I can do anything; I'm pretty much good at everything I do." I have known thousands of highly intelligent and wildly successful people, and not one would make a statement like that. Why? Because their success stemmed from being honest with themselves first.

Rank Your Priorities

There are no right or wrong answers here. This is simply about finding your flavor by identifying what priorities rank the highest for you at this point in your life. Take a moment to rank the following:

Weekends free from work

LEAST IMPORTANT 　1　2　3　4　5　MOST IMPORTANT

Flexibility with hours

LEAST IMPORTANT 　1　2　3　4　5　MOST IMPORTANT

Traveling for work

LEAST IMPORTANT 　1　2　3　4　5　MOST IMPORTANT

Having an important title

LEAST IMPORTANT 　1　2　3　4　5　MOST IMPORTANT

Working beside others

LEAST IMPORTANT 　1　2　3　4　5　MOST IMPORTANT

Working alone

LEAST IMPORTANT 　1　2　3　4　5　MOST IMPORTANT

Overseeing a project or a team

LEAST IMPORTANT 　1　2　3　4　5　MOST IMPORTANT

Being challenged mentally

LEAST IMPORTANT 　1　2　3　4　5　MOST IMPORTANT

Being challenged physically

LEAST IMPORTANT 　1　2　3　4　5　MOST IMPORTANT

Predictability and repetition

LEAST IMPORTANT   1   2   3   4   5   MOST IMPORTANT

Helping others / making a difference

LEAST IMPORTANT   1   2   3   4   5   MOST IMPORTANT

Finding Your Strengths

The best analytics for self-discovery are the ones that pinpoint things specific to *you*, not the general population. Gallup is a recognized leader in analytics, and they have a dynamic system for analyzing people quickly, summing up their strengths, and helping them understand what motivates them. Many companies, including mine, have used their CliftonStrengths talent assessment to determine who is best suited for which roles. This assessment looks at thirty-four strengths and ranks them in accordance with which strengths come naturally to a person. Research shows that when people are working in their area of strength, they use less effort and the results are generally higher quality.

When I've used assessments like these with my staff, I've better understood their strengths and what motivated each of them. Then, I was able to assign tasks that naturally suited them because I knew they could rise to the challenge. When we used the CliftonStrengths assessment, some of our employees' job duties or positions changed permanently. This was a win-win. Employees were happier with their new responsibilities, and our company benefited from them working in the positions best suited to them.

As someone who is looking for the right position or career, you will have a wonderful advantage if you know your strengths. You have a unique opportunity to identify your strengths and then preemptively highlight them during your job search, the interview process, and ultimately, your newfound employment.

Find your strengths by logging on at www.Gallup.com. Click on the CliftonStrengths 34 assessment and take the test. This is not a free test, but the results are well worth the investment. By looking at thirty-four strengths, rather than just the top five, you'll gain much more insight into what makes you tick. After you take the test, print your results and highlight the key points in the descriptions of the top ten strengths that resonate with you. Discuss these points with someone close to you.

Spend a day or two getting to know yourself on an even deeper level before moving to the next step in this book. Marinating on your results will help you fully absorb your own flavor.

How Much Money Do I Need to Make?

This is an interesting question because so many people have no idea how much money they need to pay their debts and save for the future. Personal finance is not a high school course, yet it should be required for every sixteen-year-old. Making money is easy, but saving money and managing money takes skill. Almost everyone is shocked when they get their first paycheck. For weeks, they've calculated their hourly pay and multiplied it by the number of hours they've worked. They may have already spent that money mentally. Then, they open their envelope, bank account, or payroll app and immediately think there must be some mistake because taxes were taken out and the number is far smaller than anticipated.

Much the same, even seasoned workers forget to consider the cost of variables, such as health insurance, parking fees, and gasoline prices, as they move from job to job, state to state. I have to chuckle when someone says, "Well, if I were working in New York or California, I'd be making so much more money." But they'd also be spending far more on housing, taxes, amenities, and so on.

Regardless of where you want to live or the position you want to take, you must be able to afford it, so let's start with a personal budget. This is the income you and your family need to survive and hopefully save a little, too. Grab a spiral notebook and make a conservative budget based on historical facts. Look past just rent and car payments. Assess your bank account in detail. Where did all the money go? Add up how much you spent eating out, on gas, entertainment, and even on your pet. These are real numbers, and they all need to be included.

You may be thinking that this is all so much work. You're right, it is. But it's worth it. Understanding spending habits and how much money goes out every month is a fundamental key to financial success. Failure to know and understand these facts will lead to heartache and disappointment sooner rather than later. And continued failure to focus on personal finance can lead to long-term problems and lack of future opportunities, such as owning a home.

On the contrary, truly understanding your financial status is freeing. It puts you in the driver's seat of your own future. Once you know your budget, you'll learn the bottom of what you need to make, or what it takes to keep a roof over your head, food on the table, and gas in the car. Nobody should live in their parents' basement, so strive to at least make enough to allow you to keep a one-month emergency fund in savings. As you get better at this, strive for three or six months of savings.

If you're currently not even covering expenses, you need to cut your budget and make some hard choices while you make yourself more valuable on the earning scale. You must live within your means. My mother used to ask me, "Is this a want or a need?" You'll have to ask yourself the same question as you cut back. While the internet may be a need, buying those extra channels through your cable company is not. A great resource for budgeting is Dave Ramsey's *The Total Money Makeover Workbook*. It's been around for a few years, but it's still a bestseller—for a good reason. I've used it, my children have used it, and many people I have mentored have used it—all with great success.

As you learn how to live within your means, use what you want but can't yet afford as motivation. Increasing your value to future employers will increase your means, directly improve your budget, and allow room for more of the wants on your list. It's simple math and cause and effect; this is the hard-core reality of why you must keep reading this book and working through the exercises. You can do this. And when you do, you'll be light-years ahead of where you were.

"THREE WORDS OF ADVICE FOR SOCIAL MEDIA RANTING: PROCEED WITH CAUTION!"

—Germany Kent, broadcaster and journalist

CHAPTER 3

THE WORLD'S VIEW OF YOU AND HOW TO IMPROVE IT

One year for Christmas, I received a mirror that magnifies ten times. It was something I had asked for. It wasn't until I unwrapped it, plugged it in, turned the small knob to light it up, and glared into it in horror when I realized there was so much more to me than I really wanted to see. There were wrinkles, small brown spots, and many imperfections I'd never noticed before. Why? Because I hadn't previously looked that closely at who I really was. It was an uncomfortable moment. Keep the ten-times mirror in mind as we go through this chapter. Allow yourself to see everything: the good, the bad, and the ugly.

Looking at the world's view of you is like holding a magnifying glass up to your reputation and studying it carefully. Gone are the days when a potential employer judges you solely on your résumé or your résumé and your interview. They want to know who you are and what you would bring, good or bad, to their company. Social media is a great resource for employers. This is where they start to understand your personality. While interviewing a psychologist on our *Stay Young*

America! podcast, I asked him if he could diagnose someone from their social media posts. His response was a resounding, "Absolutely!"

I could honestly list about a hundred examples of this, but the one I most often share is with a young lady we'll call Briana. She applied for a receptionist position at the luxury medical practice where I'm the CEO. We often refer to this position as the director of first impressions. Her résumé was filled with receptionist and medical clinic experience. Some of her previous positions had lasted one to two years, a few were less than a year. Normally, this would be an instant red flag, but she did have one position listed that lasted five years, so we interviewed her. Not every CEO is involved in the interviewing process, but because of our discerning clientele and the nature of our business, I want to meet all potential employees.

The normal process in our business is an internet search, a phone interview, and then two to three face-to-face interviews. For some reason, this candidate had the phone interview and an in-person interview prior to an internet search. Briana didn't have the perfect résumé, but it was decent. The interview was okay, but she didn't seem genuine. The second interview was quickly canceled after her Instagram revealed statements including: "10 Reasons Why I Hate People," "Anyone Else Have to Work with Stupid People?" and my personal favorite, "Only the Best People Can Fool 100% of the People 100% of the Time." These statements told us everything we needed to know. Can you imagine her being our director of first impressions? Crisis averted.

Your Instagram, Facebook, TikTok, and other social media sites tell a story. They're a window into what's important to you, how you handle disappointment, and your positive or negative nature. Your posts show if you're filled with gratitude or resentment, and if you're a complainer or an inspirer. Therefore, we should all take time to discover what our posts say about us. Social media posts that are inspiring, show you smiling, or show you being grateful in nature can certainly work in your favor.

Your Social Media Score

So often we grade our social media based on how many followers, likes, and reshares we have. None of that matters when it comes to employability unless you're being hired as a social media influencer. For this exercise, I want you to look only for the tone and context clues your potential employer would be looking for. As I mentioned earlier, this may be an uncomfortable exercise. Social media posts are often an outward expression of what's going on inside one's heart and mind. Take a deep breath and be honest as you scroll through your social media and score your posts below:

1. Look at your last ten posts on Facebook. How many of those ten posts were a complaint? _____

2. Look at your last ten posts on Instagram. How many of those posts were a complaint? _____

3. Look at your TikTok posts. If your general theme is educational but not political, give yourself a 0. If your posts are super silly or gross, give yourself a 5. If your posts are divisive in any way—political in nature, hitting a "hot button" for others, profane, or negative—then give yourself a 10. _____

4. If any of your social media posts on any platform contains nudity, bare shoulders, kissy faces to the camera, or any sort of promiscuous photos or sayings, add a 10 here. _____

5. If any of your social media posts says anything negative about a previous employer or coworker, give yourself 15 points here. _____

Total Your Score Here _____

Less than 5—Congratulations, your social media score is better than most. You're a positive person and don't seem to pose a threat to a future employer.

6–10—You have some work to do. Look at where you scored high and focus on those areas as you move forward. If these posts happened during a difficult time in your life and previous posts are not reflective of the same, then your score may be situational more than anything. A few high-scoring posts may trigger a future employer to look back further to see if it's a trend.

11–20—It looks as though you need to work on more than one area of your posts. This score may be a call for an attitude adjustment, especially if it's closer to 20. Take a good look at how the world sees you. Maybe ask yourself, "What do my posts tell a future employer about me?" Go back to your social media accounts and delete the posts that contributed to this score.

More than 20—My guess is you wouldn't want your parents reading your social media. It's time for a complete overhaul of how you present yourself to the world. If your score is 30 or greater, you may want to consider a coach or a therapist. They can help you better understand what's going on psychologically. Many negative or degrading posts are a symptom of a greater issue. If that statement hits a nerve, or you find offense with it, that further clarifies the need for additional help. Most employers will run from a "victim" mentality because it can be a cancer inside their organization. Be sure to avoid posts that blame others, look like excuses for your own bad behavior, or make you out to be a victim. While you should certainly take some time to clean up your social media, it may be best to delete the accounts altogether and spend some time in therapy.

LinkedIn is different from other social media platforms because it's designed to connect people in the business world. Anyone looking for a position should take some time to build their LinkedIn profile. The profile should have a professional photo—or at least one that is high enough pixels—and it should show you in something you would wear to an interview. Add your educational institutions, past work experience, and a biography highlighting your strengths. Consider LinkedIn as an extension of your résumé.

Once you have created your profile, follow a few businesses or groups that interest you, connect with people who can vouch for your professional experience, and release two to three posts a week that are relevant to your interests and the types of positions you're looking for. For example, if you're interested in a clinical research position, you may repost a few recent studies and mention what you found interesting about the conclusion of the research. Likewise, if you're interested in logistics, posts about supply-chain changes, fuel prices, or anything related to transportation would be appropriate. The goal here is to show that you have a shared interest with those who may be interviewing you.

Education and Influence

One thing every employer loves to see is initiative. That's why posting content that is educational in nature can work in your favor. You don't have to know everything, but sharing the things you do know about will go a long way. This is where content creation comes in. Anyone can create content, and those who do it well will benefit from it either directly or indirectly. If you choose to use AI for content creation, be sure to read through, edit, fact-check, and give the final product a personal touch before you post it.

I once spoke to an electrician who wanted to change companies in hopes of advancement from within a larger company. My advice to him was simple. Create YouTube videos about electricity. The fifteen videos he created were aimed at the consumer and were simply about electrical safety within the home, addressing questions he had been asked frequently by previous customers. He listed his YouTube channel on his résumé. That initiative afforded him not only the interview with the larger company, but he was also hired and paid extra for creating similar videos for the new company. What's the lesson here? He didn't have to be the most intelligent or tenured electrician; he just had to show initiative and promise.

YouTube and other platforms are a tremendous way to expand upon your résumé, showing future employers you have other skills, such as communicating or teaching. A few other great platforms worth mentioning are personal blogs, being a guest on other people's blogs, podcasting, being a guest on other podcasts, or writing articles for traditional or online trade magazines.

Personal websites and blogs are easier to create than ever thanks to platforms like Wix. The setup can be done within a few hours, and you don't have to be a computer guru. These sorts of user-friendly platforms are also little to no cost, so there's no reason not to have one. As you grow professionally, so can your website. You may say, "I don't have time." My response is, "You need to find the time." This is one of those significant return-on-investment items because it gives employers so much information about you, and it's information you control. Your blog is the perfect place to express your interests, knowledge, and skills. A personal website shows initiative. Remember, employers love initiative. Regardless of industry, those at the top are almost always there because they have a proactive approach to life.

Being a guest on other people's blogs is another great way to expand your reach and gain credibility. If you want to advance your career in the financial world, look for blogs about finance and then pitch a story idea to them. Guest blogs usually have a few caveats:

1. Content should be original and not posted elsewhere.
2. Proofread your post and ensure it is free of typos and uses proper grammar.
3. The blogger will expect you to share the article so their blog reaches an extended audience.

Podcasting isn't for everyone, and it can be time-consuming. If you have the gift of gab and enjoy entertaining, it's worth looking into.

The Libsyn platform is a place to start. Before investing in podcasting equipment, take time to do their tutorials or watch other educational videos on the topic. I also strongly recommend listening to other podcasts with a discerning ear. What works? What doesn't? Why do you like certain ones and dislike others? Before jumping off the deep end with your own podcast, be a guest on someone else's. Then, go back and listen to yourself. Do you speak clearly and concisely? What do you need to improve upon? If you find yourself using filler words like "um" or "ah," join a local Toastmasters so you can learn the art of communication in a safe environment. Once you're ready, create something you'd like to listen to, something you find interesting, and something future employers would be impressed with. Podcasts can be linked to your website and shared on your social media. They are a powerful way to build instant credibility.

I often say podcasts are for extroverts and article writing is for introverts, but the people who can do both are rare gems. Maybe you're one of those rare gems, or maybe you prefer to just do one or the other. Writing articles is an easy way to show the world you have something to offer. Medium is an online publishing platform that allows you to publish your blog or start a publication of your articles to which others can subscribe. The writers on Medium include those new to writing and award-winning authors. It's a community that has a free version and a paid subscription version. The best part about Medium is that people go there to write, but they also go there to read, so it's a great place to establish a fan base for your work.

As you read through this chapter, I hope you have a better understanding of how your presence, or lack thereof, relates to your employability. No matter where you are in your journey, there is always room for improvement. Improvement comes one step at a time, and it's a process. You don't have to do everything in this chapter all at once. Start by cleaning up your social media, then move on to building a LinkedIn profile. Once those are complete, find one or two ways to create content. Go to www.StopWhiningStartWorking.com to download my free thirty-day, step-by-step Revive My Reputation worksheet. It's easy to follow and takes you through the process one day at a time. The best part about doing this work is that it not only makes you more employable but also improves your self-esteem. You're starting to become the leader you were meant to be, so keep pushing forward.

"THE CHALLENGE OF LIFE, I HAVE FOUND, IS TO BUILD A RÉSUMÉ THAT DOESN'T SIMPLY TELL A STORY ABOUT WHAT YOU WANT TO BE, BUT IT'S A STORY ABOUT WHO YOU WANT TO BE."

—Oprah Winfrey

CHAPTER 4

WRITING A RÉSUMÉ THAT ROCKS

Imagine your résumé is just an oversized business card. How many business cards have you collected over the years that landed in your purse or wallet until you eventually threw them out? When we're handed someone's business card, we ask ourselves, "Would I use this person's services? Do I trust them?" When you send out a résumé, those are the same questions potential employers will ask themselves. It's less about filling a chair than it is about filling that chair with the right person, the person who will service the company in a meaningful and respectful way.

Many well-meaning experts will tell you there are hard and fast rules about writing a résumé. Some will say they need to be only one page, some will say to list only your last two employers, and others will tell you to make it as long as possible and to throw in everything you've ever done since the first grade. Who's right? Well, that depends. Not the answer you were expecting, I'm sure. Many one-page résumés have landed great jobs, and so have many three-page résumés.

This is where the "service the company in a meaningful way" statement comes into play. Your first step in landing a job is to understand what an employer is interested in. They are tuned into the only station that matters: WIIFM (What's in It for Me). Their job is not to tell you how smart you are, how proud they are of all your accomplishments, or even to critique your résumé. Their sole job is to scan résumés to determine who makes it to the next level—the phone or in-person interview. You earn that next step by carefully crafting a résumé showing you have something to offer their company.

I named this chapter "Writing a Résumé That Rocks" because you want to rock their world in some sort of way. They need to see your résumé, pause, and then conclude that you are worth their time. Your résumé is not just your large business card; it's your commercial. You're the product, and they're the consumer. Once you understand this concept and shift your perspective, the rest is simply about mechanics.

An editor position with a publisher would require a different type of résumé than a creative director with a nonprofit children's camp would. The publisher would be looking for a résumé that was clean, tidy, and perhaps black and white, both physically and metaphorically. They're looking for facts and your ability to be succinct. But any position that has to do with creativity will want just the opposite. Such a résumé is more of a glimpse into your creative portfolio. In creative jobs, there is a sort of unspoken expectation that your personality and skills should shine through on the page. Using graphic elements and color are not just acceptable, they may move your résumé to the top of the stack.

The publishing company may not care that the editor's first job was a nanny, but you can bet the nonprofit children's camp would. Why? Because they will see value in that experience; it's a clue that the candidate likes children, and they know how to govern themselves and manage their time. However, if someone is applying for the editor position and wrote for their university newspaper, even if it was a decade ago, it's still relevant information and should be included. The lesson here is to view all the contents of your résumé and your past experiences through the eyes of the potential employer. This may mean you craft one résumé and tweak it ever so slightly depending on the position you're applying for.

If you find yourself writing your first résumé, or your first résumé in a long time, you may not know where to start. You can spend money on résumé templates, but it's not necessary. Most people have Microsoft Word, and it has plenty of résumé templates that you can use. The following are a few things to remember when writing your résumé:

1. List your employers in reverse chronological order, with the most recent first. Include company name, company address (at least city and state), position held, and dates of employment for each. List months and years, not just years. If you're still employed, be sure to put your start date and then a dash before the word "present" next to your current employer.

2. Include educational accolades with the most important one first. For example, if you have a master's, a bachelor's, and some certifications, list them in that order. If you earned a degree, list the year, but if you're still in school, list the expected completion date. This is also a great place to list things like making the dean's list, graduating magna cum laude, or your current grade point average.

3. Community involvement and volunteer work should be listed if current or in the last couple of years. If it's more than two years old, leave it off *unless* that experience could somehow strengthen your candidacy for the position. If you have no community involvement, this is an area you should be working on. If your community involvement is political, you may want to leave it off your résumé.

4. Don't be afraid to list your hobbies. These usually go at the end of the résumé or off to the side. Hobbies are a great way to connect with others who may be interviewing you.

Preparing to Apply

To fully understand what an employer wants, you must first do your homework. I've created a PEP (Potential Employer Preparation) tool for you to use below. You can get a printable version of this form on www.StopWhiningStartWorking.com. This form will help you identify clues about the company's culture, the position you're applying for, and their expectations. You will need a new form for each company, and you can reference these sheets as you move through the interview process. The PEP sheet will prepare you in ways that will get you noticed. Doing your homework prior to an interview will also help you become their most prepared candidate and, thus, the most memorable.

PEP

Company Name:_____

Company Website:_____

Contact Name:_____

Contact Email/Phone:_____

Position Applying for:_____

Company Mission Statement:_____

_____

Company Vision Statement:_____

_____

Key Words in Ad:_____

_____

Tone of the Company's Social Media Posts:_____

_____

_____

Notes from Any Pertinent News or Recent Press Releases:

_____

_____

The first PEP you complete may seem onerous or time-consuming, but the more of these you do, the faster you'll be able to complete them. Think about interviews in the past and if you were nervous. Maybe your anxiety was because you had no idea what to expect out of the interview, and you had no idea what they expected out of you. The information you place on this form will arm you with critical data that will help you feel prepared. Preparation and information are the antidotes to performance anxiety.

You can usually find the company's mission and vision statements on their website. As you write them down, look for essential words. Consider these words to be golden nuggets. They just told you what they are as a company and what they want to become. If their statements and your abilities and personality align, that's a point you'll want to make. How do you do that? By making sure your résumé, cover letter, and interview mirror those statements in the tone you use. That doesn't mean you use the exact same words, but it does mean you convey the same feelings and ideas. For example, if a company's mission includes being involved in the community, emphasize your community involvement. Likewise, if their vision is about growth, share a time when your skills helped a company, club, or group grow and expand.

The previous chapter discussed how social media can give employers insight into who you are and your general attitude. The same is true when the tables are turned. A company's social media (if they have any) is a great way to check out its culture. Are the posts fun and whimsical, or are they serious and industry-driven? Take notes because this will often give you an idea of how personable the interview may be—or not be.

Companies often go through transitional phases. Depending on the size of a company, these changes may play out in the news or can be discovered through their own press releases. Start by going to their website and looking for tabs marked News for press releases. Afterward, go to Google, toggle over to the News tab, and search the full company name in quotes. This information is fair game when it comes to the interview. For example, if you see that there has been a major shakeup in leadership, it's okay to ask how the company is adapting to the new leadership or how things are expected to change. Some news stories may be a turnoff. It's okay to decide a company is not the right fit for you because of layoffs, investigations, or other negative press. Remember, knowledge is power, and you're looking for the right job just as much as they're looking for the right candidate.

"OUTSTANDING PEOPLE HAVE ONE THING IN COMMON: AN ABSOLUTE SENSE OF MISSION."

—Zig Ziglar, author and motivational speaker

CHAPTER 5

COVER LETTERS THAT STAND OUT

Think of a cover letter as your first conversation with your potential employer. Your résumé is your oversized business card, and the letter accompanying it is your handshake and friendly introduction. Using this analogy, consider what would impress you about someone you just met. I doubt that a well-rehearsed, five-minute rant about how great they are would leave you wanting more.

Believe it or not, I have had a few candidates say they didn't include a cover letter because they weren't sure what a cover letter was. Wow. I remember when these sorts of things were taught in high school. Even if the candidate didn't know how to write one based on experience, they could have done a quick internet search. You, too, can do a quick internet search for "cover letter" to get an idea of the format. You can also use a Microsoft Word template or follow the simple guidelines below.

Cover Letter Formatting 101

DO use 1-inch margins and an 11- or 12-point, easy-to-read font like Arial, Times New Roman, Calibri, or Verdana.

DO address your cover letter to the person who will be hiring or interviewing you. You then address them with "Dear" followed by either first and last name, or Mr. or Ms. first and last name, or Mr. or Ms. last name only. (Don't put Mrs. unless you know for a fact they are married.) With the current political climate, however, it will probably be safest to use first and last name and leave off the honorifics of Mr. and Ms. However, if you are being interviewed by someone with a PhD or medical degree, you will absolutely want to be sure to have Dr. in front of their name.

DON'T be generic. *Never* address it "To Whom It May Concern" or "Dear Sir" or "Dear Madam." If you don't know who will be interviewing you, call and ask. It's okay to tell them you need the name for the cover letter you're preparing. Generic salutations scream lazy and disinterested.

DO format the header correctly. An example is listed below:

<Your Name>

<Your Street Address>

<Your City, State>

<Your Phone Number>

<Your Email>

<Your LinkedIn Profile> (**DO** hyperlink this if sending digitally)

<Your Website or Blog> (if you have this completed, and it is presentable)

<Date>

<Name of Person Interviewing or Hiring Manager>

<Title of Person Listed Above>

<Legal Name of the Company> (**DON'T** abbreviate this)

<Company Street Address>

\<Company City, State\>

NOTE: If you're using a creative cover letter template, it's fine to have your name and return address listed somewhere else on that page in accordance with the template design.

DO open with a recent accomplishment you're proud of. This should be something related to your current or previous job. But if you're fresh out of college, use a story about a lesson you learned, a goal you accomplished, or service work that taught you a life lesson or skill. Keep this to no more than four sentences.

DO your research and make the next paragraph about the interviewer's professional accomplishments, or better yet, what you like about their company. This should be specific and show the person interviewing you that you did your homework and have a sincere interest.

DO make mention of recent company accolades. For example, it may have been awarded "Best Places to Work," or it may have had a recent acquisition or reported positive earnings.

DON'T drop names unless it's legitimate. I once had an applicant tell me someone in town had referred them. When I asked that person for a personal reference, they said they had met them, but they had not actually referred them. Just because you have a mutual connection online or a chance meeting, that does not constitute a legitimate relationship and certainly not a referral. But if you have been referred, by all means, name-drop. Better yet, ask that person if they can write you a letter of recommendation. I love letters of recommendation because they save me and my team from playing phone tag with the reference.

DO end by describing why you're the best fit for the position. This closing paragraph is literally your closer. It's meant to sell you to them. List your passion for the position, what skills make you the best fit, and other outstanding qualities they need to know. Be specific.

DO make the last paragraph two sentences. The first one should simply be a statement of gratitude, and the last sentence should always be a trigger for action, such as "I look forward to hearing from you" or "I look forward to a more formal introduction."

DO use "Sincerely" or "Respectfully" when closing your letter. Type your name below, leaving enough room to drop in an electric version of your signature. If you will be printing the letter, just leave enough space to sign above your printed name.

In some cases, the cover letter must be typed into a company's online application form and may even have character space limits. If so, you can leave off the header information and get to the meat of the letter. Avoid the temptation to be too informal. Be professional yet engaging.

If you're applying through a job search site like Indeed or ZipRecruiter, take a moment to understand how to upload both a résumé and a cover letter. If you are still having trouble, combine both the cover letter and résumé into one file and upload it as a single document. Be sure to label it accordingly.

One thing that is often overlooked by applicants is the file name. Never send a résumé or cover letter that's labeled in an informal way. Over the years, my colleagues and I have laughed over a few file names, like "Moms_best_resume," "CleanedUpResume," and "Resume Without Bad Jobs Listed." Instead, name the files like this: j.smith_resume or j.smith_cover_letter. It's okay to add a tag to the end of the file name, especially the cover letter, so you're sure to send them the right one. You can tag them by number and have a master list of which cover letter number goes with which company, or you can add initials. For example, if you are applying to Coca-Cola, you could name your file like this: j.smith_cover_letter_CC.

Unless a company specifically states that they do not want a cover letter, you should send one. Many people think it's best only to send a cover letter if it's requested; they may feel it's outdated, or they think it's unnecessary. Don't fall into that mindset. Hard work and manners are timeless and still appreciated.

Don't just take my word for it when it comes to cover letters; follow the research. ResumeLab, a software company dedicated to helping people build better résumés, surveyed two hundred people in the hiring seat. These included recruiters, managers, and human resources (HR) specialists, who overwhelmingly agreed that cover letters play a significant role in their hiring decisions. They also agreed, at the rate of 83 percent, that a good cover letter could even convince them to interview a candidate with a less-than-ideal résumé.

The survey also collected great information on the mindset of those who hire. While job posts that require letters to accompany the résumé are around 60 percent, nearly 74 percent of respondents said they prefer the applicant send one. It's shocking that out of all the job seekers applying, the average number of candidates who take the time to send in a letter is as low as 35 percent. Imagine how your résumé, accompanied by a great cover letter, will stand out!

Decision-makers like me and other business executives I know appreciate it when an applicant writes a letter with a purpose. That purpose, besides explaining why they would be an ideal candidate, may shed light on the accompanying résumé. For example, if there is a gap in employment or a recent demographic relocation, this is a great opportunity to explain it and get ahead of unconscious biases the hiring manager may have.

If you're thinking this all sounds like a lot of work—you're right. But it's not busywork; it's productive, and it's work that will pay off in the long run. Your goal is not to be a candidate, it's to be the best candidate. And the best candidates always work hard for that title. My mother gave me great advice that I passed down to my own children: "You can either hope to get the highest grade in the class, or you can set the bar for the A."

"COURAGE STARTS WITH SHOWING UP AND LETTING OURSELVES BE SEEN."

—Brené Brown, University of Houston research professor, best-selling author, and speaker

CHAPTER 6

WHERE TO LOOK FOR JOBS

Online job boards are a great place to look for your first job or your next career move, but I say that with a caveat. Searching for, applying for, and landing a job from a job board is not an instant process. In this world of Amazon Prime and lightning-speed access to just about everything, it may be hard to understand that job hunting is not for the faint of heart. It takes work, follow-up, and perseverance.

Remember you are looking for the *right* job, not just any job. The decision-makers are looking for the *right* candidate, not just any candidate. Imagine for a moment that the hiring manager is a fisherman. They gather their tackle and drift out on the water, hoping to catch a largemouth bass and nothing else. Hours go by, and they reel in ten other types of fish but no largemouth bass, so they dock their boat and go out again the next day. Now, imagine you are that largemouth bass looking for just the right bait. You swim past hook after hook, but nobody is fishing with worms except that one fisherman. The problem is that you are on the opposite side of the lake. You just must keep swimming, and they must keep fishing until you find each other.

Being a job seeker on a job board can be a game of hurry up and wait. You need to apply while the job is fresh, yet you may be waiting quite some time to hear back. GetHired reports that average hiring processes can take up to six weeks. Likewise, Glassdoor reports that many employers take an average of twenty-three days to respond to job applicants. On average, larger companies take longer than smaller ones when it comes to scheduling interviews. Meanwhile, you're chewing your nails off, wondering if they will ever respond. The Human Capital Institute reported that 75 percent of job applicants never hear back once they apply. Don't get discouraged—even if you don't hear back after following up. Just keep swimming. You only need to land one right job, not all those you apply for.

Board Games

Not all job boards are the same, and they play by different rules. To further understand the most common job boards, let's look at who owns and runs them. This exercise should help you better understand why being active on more than one board is important. All of these companies compete for business, and they won't have the same positions listed. In the past, we have used all of these but not at the same time.

Indeed is owned by Recruit Holdings Co., Ltd., a Japanese employment and staffing company. The current CEO of Indeed is Chris Hyams. He has held several leadership roles at Indeed since joining the company in 2006. It's a highly technical site with stable leadership.

LinkedIn is owned by Microsoft, which they acquired in 2016 for $26 billion. The CEO of LinkedIn is Ryan Roslansky, and he has been in his position since 2020. Can you imagine becoming the CEO of LinkedIn in 2020, the year the world turned upside down? I can't, but since he is still there at the time of writing this, he must be doing a great job.

Monster is owned by Randstad North America, a global HR and staffing firm based in the Netherlands. The CEO of Monster is Scott Gutz. He became CEO in 2018 after Monster was acquired by Randstad.

ZipRecruiter is a privately held company owned primarily by institutional investors. They have raised over $200 million in funding, and almost everyone has heard of their "needle in a haystack" commercials. The CEO and cofounder of ZipRecruiter is Ian Siegel, who, along with two other cofounders, helped launch the company in 2010. It's safe to say that as CEO and a cofounder, he has a particular interest in the company's success.

Indeed is arguably the most popular job search site, and they aggregate listings from thousands of company websites and other job sites. Employers can list for free here or pay to have optimized listings. Some of their strengths include their powerful search functions and filters. They also have a résumé database, which I strongly recommend. The database allows employers to search for candidates they want to invite to apply. Some decision-makers will buy access to résumé so they can pick and choose rather than rely on candidates to find them. Most candidates find it easy to apply through Indeed.

Employers tend to like Indeed because they can request skills assessments. Note: If a job posting sends you a skills assessment, take it. If you want to be a star, go in and take multiple assessments to add to your résumé. Only list assessments you score proficient or higher on. One drawback I have found on Indeed is that some candidates find it harder to upload their cover letter along with their résumé. But it can be done, and I have received plenty of cover letters through that site.

Monster is a well-known job site that offers a broad range of job postings across industries and career levels. I like that they have résumé help and career resources and advice for candidates. Take advantage of their expertise. Monster also lets you explore career paths and required skills and experience for jobs you may be interested in, which is a nice feature. Wondering what the average pay would be for a specific position? They also have a salary-data tool.

LinkedIn is primarily a professional social network rather than a traditional job board, but more and more companies are finding candidates here. Many of their jobs listed tend to be more senior level or advanced in specialization, which is great if you have experience and a hefty résumé. LinkedIn has a strong focus on making connections and networking with others. That gives you an advantage as a member and a job seeker because you can play the Kevin Bacon game and find your six degrees of separation. Someone you know is connected to someone who knows someone and so on.

The key to LinkedIn is to have a robust personal page. Your photo and bio should be professional, and you'll need to connect with others to show that you're actively participating on the platform. Also, be sure to follow associations related to your profession or desired profession. I would avoid following political or activist groups. LinkedIn has a unique feature that enables you to ask others to endorse you for certain skills. Take advantage of that feature. If you apply for a position through this site, the person who listed the job will almost always check your LinkedIn profile before doing anything else. Imagine how impressed they would be to see that you are well-connected and endorsed by others for the exact skills they want.

ZipRecruiter uses matching algorithms to recommend relevant job opportunities, which makes it easier for you. Their mobile-optimized application process has a one-click apply tool, but don't get too click happy. Make sure you're following the exact application instructions for the job post and including a personal note—or even better, a cover letter. Candidates like ZipRecruiter because it provides status updates on applications and has a number of resources to aid in the job search journey.

The most effective site for you depends on your industry, experience level, and whether you prioritize networking, job listings, application tracking, or recruiting outreach. Don't fall into the false narrative that a certain platform is useless; they all have benefits and weaknesses. Utilizing multiple platforms is often most effective, regardless of what type of position you're looking for. You may even stumble upon a position you weren't searching for but find intriguing. Sometimes those turn out to be the best and bring life-changing surprises.

Regardless of which platforms you decide to use, be certain to get as specific as possible by utilizing advanced search filters. You can search by title, location, date of posting, company name, salary range, job type, and more to narrow your search. Look at your specific skill set and search for jobs that list your skills under their list of requirements. Keep in mind the fish and fisherman analogy. You're using search terms to get closer and closer to the fisherman using the right bait.

Being proactive is so important when it comes to using online job boards. Set up job alerts that either text or email you when matches are listed. This will speed up the process of your response. Some companies have settings that close a job listing after so many applicants, while others may manually turn the job off after the applicants start stacking up.

While this chapter focused on four of the major sites, there are others, such as CareerBuilder, SimplyHired, and more. You can do your own research to find job boards that are industry-specific or otherwise, but below are a few examples:

- TheLadders.com—Used by 100,000-plus job seekers, many of whom are executive and upper-level managers.
- AllRetailJobs.com—This includes all jobs associated with the retail industry.
- Dice.com—Information technology and engineering professionals can find permanent and contract work here.
- eFinancialCareers.com—Banking, technology, and finance positions are listed on this site.
- JobsInLogistics.com—Supply-chain and logistics positions are listed here.
- FlexJobs.com—If remote or part-time work is important to you, this is a great place to find all kinds of jobs, from entry-level to fractional executive.

As you post, apply, and reapply, I wish you all the best. Keep your chin up and keep swimming. Don't just take the first job you find; stay dedicated to finding the right job. Remember, everyone who currently has a position they love was once in your same position. They found theirs, and you will find yours, too.

WIN THE ALGORITHM WAR

Online application sites are highly automated. Since there are hundreds of thousands of people applying every day, job sites use algorithms to weed out applicants who don't meet the description set forth by the employers. If you're not hearing back when applying online, it's highly likely that nobody's seeing your résumé. You can win the war against those pesky (yet necessary) algorithms by beating them at their own game. Below is a list of popular apps and tools that can help you rewrite and tailor your résumé to specific job requirements:

Jobscan: Upload your résumé and a job posting, and Jobscan will provide a match-rate analysis. It also gives you tips to better align your résumé content to make you a better match.

Novoresume: A useful résumé builder that has a "Job Description Analyzer" feature that suggests relevant skills and phrases to include based on the job post description.

Resume Genius: In addition to templates, this site offers tips and tools to customize your résumé for different roles and industries. It's a great place to start forming your résumé.

Resumob: This app puts artificial intelligence to work for you. It analyzes job descriptions and automatically rewrites your résumé to match the requirements and include relevant keywords. When using this, be sure that the rewritten résumé is an accurate representation of your skills and experience before submitting it.

Rezi: A résumé optimization tool that identifies keywords from job descriptions and suggests updates to your résumé to improve your match score. Not as advanced as some other apps but a useful tool, no doubt.

VisualCV: This résumé builder allows you to create multiple tailored versions of your résumé and easily swap sections to match different job postings. Perfect for people with multiple skill sets.

"NETWORKING IS THE NO. 1 UNWRITTEN RULE OF SUCCESS IN BUSINESS."

—Sallie Krawcheck, CEO and cofounder of Ellevest, a digital financial adviser for women, and the most powerful woman on Wall Street

CHAPTER 7

THE UNADVERTISED POSITION

Y ou've done so much great work by now. You're prepared to start actively looking for the position that best matches your needs, and you've begun to look in all the obvious places. Nothing you've searched for seems right. There may be a company you really want to work for, but you never see them advertising their positions. That's because some companies choose not to advertise their job openings to the masses. This is especially true when it comes to professional-level positions.

Atta Tarki, author of *Evidence-Based Recruiting* and founder of executive search firm ECA Partners, agrees that a high number of all jobs are never advertised on traditional job boards. His advice is to check job boards once a week. Pick a particular day of the week to search and apply. But try to timebox this activity as most candidates tend to spend too much time on job boards. He also counsels his clients to seek out recruiters who are industry-specific and follow up with them every six weeks to stay on their radar. Then, spend the rest of the time networking. A soft introduction is always better than a cold one.

Recruitment consultants are often the first to know when a job opening may be coming. Because they have strong relationships with the companies they work for, they are often brought into the loop very early. For example, someone in human resources may have caught wind of a disgruntled employee or heard from upper management that they're thinking of making a change. Executive recruiters are also tipped off when a senior executive is considering retirement. With the anticipation that a replacement may take time, companies trust their recruiting firms to start looking quietly rather than sending out some sort of official announcement.

Although many companies use recruiters, there are still plenty that don't. For those, it's up to the job seeker to contact the company directly. According to Tarki, many people make the mistake of reaching out to the HR department to see if the company is hiring. Instead, it's best to connect with someone within the department in which you want to work, specifically someone who has decision-making power. For example, if you're looking for a position in marketing, the chief marketing officer (CMO) or VP of marketing would be the best person to reach out to. They would know the needs of their department better than anyone else. LinkedIn is a great resource for identifying people in certain positions at specific companies.

If you're a professional in a particular industry or looking to enter a different industry with your skill set, find ways to bump into the people you need to meet. This can be done by attending seminars they're likely to attend, looking for mutual connections on social media, or asking around at church or in social circles.

Earlier in this book, I emphasized the benefits of community involvement. There are people in your community right now who know the people you need to meet. The six degrees of separation is a real thing, and I have seen it work time and time again. Somebody knows somebody who knows somebody else, all of which will eventually lead you to the right person. It takes a bit of investigative work, but it can be fun, especially when you see it work out.

Build Relationships

Civic and nonprofit organizations are breeding grounds for future leaders. Older and wiser people are always excited to help those searching for ways to better their lives. I can't tell you the number of long-term relationships I have formed through joining the chamber of commerce, volunteering for nonprofits or at church, or helping with local events. I've benefited from those relationships, and in turn, others have benefited from my help.

Building relationships with those in the community or with a recruiter gives you a great advantage. Everyone needs a good cheerleader, an accountability partner, or a group of people to connect with during the job search process. As you build these relationships, there are some rules. First, don't appear desperate. It's okay to be eager to work, but never make someone feel it's their job to fix your unemployment. The second rule is that you can't just be a taker. Bring something to the table. Help others along the way. Be a connector of people, offer solutions you may have to their problems, and be engaged and present. Never, ever, just be a taker.

Home In on Your Expertise

Sometimes the unadvertised job is unadvertised because the company didn't know they needed someone in that position. This is how many people drift into a position simply because they have a unique skill. We often see this with technological advancements. A decade ago, many companies had someone in the office handle their social media (if they had anyone). Today, social media manager is a real title and a forty-hours-a-week position. The same is true for cybersecurity officers and many other positions.

If you find that you have a unique skill and it solves a unique problem, you may have a unique opportunity! This is where your relationships can help you get the introductions. If you can explain to a company that you will add value by eliminating a pain point, then they may give you a chance to prove yourself. Know your skills, polish them, and promote yourself as someone they can't live without.

Are you not sure what you have to offer? Maybe you have skills outside of those in your current or past positions. A friend of mine taught himself how to make an app. He watched countless hours of videos, read books, and studied code. His purpose was to help him track his own time better. While plenty of apps were out there for time management, none worked with his unique scheduling issues. A couple of years later, he suffered his third layoff from the same industry. Deflated emotionally and financially depleted, he started looking at changing industries altogether. During a casual conversation, he mentioned his success in creating his app. At that moment, it was as if the light bulb went off inside his head. He realized he had a skill he had never monetized. Within months, he was an app developer at a large corporation, making more than double his previous salary.

Dr. Stephie Althouse, CEO of The Brilliance Mine, is an expert dedicated to helping people find their brilliance so they can monetize it and live the life they deserve. She believes everyone has knowledge and wisdom unique to their own combinations of experience. If you're ready to change careers or find the gold within your own brain, you can take an introduction to her Brilliance Mining Course for free at www. TheBrilliancemineAcademy.com.

Follow the News

Press releases are a great way to determine which companies are growing or changing. Follow the news on an app, by watching the local news, or through social media. Business journals are also a great place to get the scoop on company news. The best part about press releases and business journals is the name-dropping. Look for who's quoted, what their title is, and who and what they're talking about. Many press releases also contain a nugget of gold that's often overlooked. In the About section following the meat of the press release, there is often an employee's name and email address. That address leaves a clue about how the company creates its email addresses. For example, if the contact for the press release is Mary Smith and her email is listed as smith.m@ TheCompanyName.com, and you've recently discovered that the person you've wanted to contact at the company is named Mark Jones, chances are you can reach him at jones.m@TheCompanyName.com.

While news about a company can help you discover opportunities, it can also help you avoid potential disasters. If the company you've been pursuing announces layoffs, you may want to shift your focus. Nobody wants to jump on a sinking ship. Likewise, if the company has had legal trouble or bad press, you may not want your name associated with it. There are plenty of other opportunities that don't end in heartache.

Company websites will often have a page dedicated to company news. Not only will you find helpful information about their business milestones, but you can often see news of leadership changes, promotions, and new hires. Read through these with a discerning eye as they offer clues. Do they promote within or hire from the outside? How often are they turning over their leadership? When it comes to the job search, use your best detective skills to uncover hidden clues.

"THE MOST BEAUTIFUL THING YOU CAN WEAR IS CONFIDENCE."

—Blake Lively, actress

CHAPTER 8

NAILING THE INTERVIEW

Some people find it difficult to talk about themselves for fear of sounding like a narcissist. And unless you're from the South, where we'll talk to just about anyone, you probably prefer not to have meaningful conversations with strangers. Considering that an interview requires both talking about yourself and forming meaningful conversations with someone you just met, it's safe to say that very few people look forward to a job interview. So if you're nervous about this stage of the job search, you're not alone. Here's the good news: I don't recall anyone ever dying from a job interview. Everyone who has a job went through this process and passed the test! You can, too.

The best way to get over the stress of doing something you don't want to do is to do that thing again and again until the emotion has no more power over you. It's time to get out of your comfort zone. Practice talking about yourself in meaningful ways with those you trust. Ask friends and family members to ask you open-ended questions about you, your life, and your job history. As you answer their questions, work on perfecting your responses so you no longer need to think about what you're going to say. Remember that this is your story, and nobody knows it better than you do. You are the expert on you, and the prospective employer is simply on a fact-finding mission and has come to you, the expert, to learn more.

Interview answers should always be factual, but they do not have to be a tell-all dissertation about your life. Leave out the fact that you worked with Krystal, the woman in the cubical next to you at your last job, who drove you crazy because she spoke too loudly and is the reason you eventually had to leave. Why? Because they will not be sympathetic to your complaint. Instead, they will hear that you have trouble getting along with people and have a low tolerance, so much so that you're still complaining about her. Every word you say speaks to who you are as a person and shows them the type of employee they would be getting if they hired you. Your words are the clues that will make or break the interview. While your words are your choice, you should always choose wisely.

Don't complain about previous employers or coworkers either directly or indirectly. Ever. Too many people choose to take up precious interview time going on and on about how much smarter they are compared to the people they worked with or how they did all the work and everyone else just sat around at their past job. Those types of remarks are huge red flags for an employer. You might ask, "How could they be bad if they're true?" If you say these things, even if you believe they are true, you just give them verbal confirmation that you are not a team player and you do not possess leadership skills. A good leader can rally the troops and encourage teamwork. True leaders are always part of the solution and look to encourage rather than criticize. Even if the job you're applying for doesn't require you to lead a team, all employers are looking for leadership qualities. Why? Because you must be able to lead yourself.

The words you use in your interview have far more power than those typed on your résumé. As you practice your interview questions and answers with friends and family, avoid words and phrases with negative connotations. Instead, choose positive ones. For example, responses that start with "I can" or "I'm happy to" will be much more well-received than those that start with "I don't" or "I prefer not to."

If you're asked about something you don't know how to do, it's better to answer in a positive way: "I'm happy to learn Excel, and I can do that on my own time through tutorials" is a far better answer than, "I never had to use Excel before, so I don't really know how it works." The latter response will most likely be the end of your progress in the interview process. To the contrary, the first response, the positive one, still leaves the door open for further discussion because it shows that you have initiative. Skills can be taught, but personality cannot. People are almost always hired for their skills and almost always fired for their lack of interpersonal skills or failure to show initiative. The companies that put more emphasis on the personality style of the employee they seek to hire, and then invest in their skills, almost always have more success.

While you're practicing the interview process, be sure to make it a two-way conversation. Think of good questions you can ask as the interview progresses. A good candidate can balance being interesting while still being interested. This is how you improve your likability factor. People hire people they like. Too much time spent on being interested can leave you with little time to sell yourself as a candidate. Taking it to the extreme can also sound like a reverse interview. Likewise, spending too much time convincing them you're the most outstanding candidate and wildly interesting will make you come across as a narcissist.

Balance starts with you doing your research before the interview. Use your PEP sheet to formulate the questions you could ask about the company or the interviewer. Company history, LinkedIn profiles of the leadership and the person interviewing you, and recent press releases are perfect places to start. The more you know before you go, the more empowered you'll be.

Over the years, I've had job candidates comment on my *Stay Young America!* podcast episodes, the accolades that our company has received, and the special interests of our practitioners. Those candidates almost always make it to the second interview because they showed interest in us, our company, and working with us in the future. These candidates also knew enough about the company and the position to explain in detail why they would be the best candidate. They used this information to frame how they would be a great addition to the team.

Practice Questions

Use the following questions as you practice. People who take this exercise seriously will decrease their anxiety about the interview process. Remember, nothing squashes nerves quite like preparation. There will be plenty of unknown factors when you enter an interview, but how you will answer the questions doesn't need to be one of them.

Questions for you, asked by the interviewer:

1. What was it about this position that interested you?

2. How do your skills align with those required for this position?

3. What do you already know about our company?

4. Why do you have an interest in what we do as a company?

5. Where do you see yourself in five years? How do we fit into that plan?

6. Tell me about a time you failed. What did you learn from that experience?

7. Tell me about a time you were proud of a decision you made.

8. What is the hardest thing you've ever done?

9. Give me five to seven adjectives family and friends would use to describe you. (I always love it when someone lists at least one neutral or negative adjective. I once had a candidate say her mother would call her stubborn. I hired her. Not because she was stubborn, but because she was honest and real with her answers.)

10. Out of all the candidates, why should I hire you?

Questions for them, asked by you, the interviewee:

1. How long have you been here, and what made you interview with this company?

2. What do you like best about working here?

3. Every company has challenges. What challenges is this company currently facing?

4. I read you went to college at _____. How did your education and experience there help you with this company?

5. Tell me a bit about the company culture.

6. What challenges have you had filling and keeping people in similar positions to the one I'm applying for?

7. What attributes do you feel are the most important for this position?

8. I reviewed your company mission (or vision) statement. Let me ask you about _____. How are you applying _____ to your everyday operations?

9. I've read the company's history. Do you foresee a continued growth curve? (Adjust this question according to what's applicable.)

10. Tell me a bit more about the company's hiring process.

If you want to make a great impression and be a stellar candidate, you need to put the time in, long before your interview starts. I mentioned earlier that your answers are clues for them to determine the type of person you are. Turnabout is always fair play, so use the answers they give you as clues about them. Look for ways you can get them to talk. Everyone's favorite voice to listen to is their own. The more they talk, the better they'll feel the interview went. The more they talk about themselves or the things they care about, the more they will naturally trust you. It sounds odd, but people bond through sharing stories, and many studies over many years back this up. Use it to your advantage and be sure you use it in balance with the questions they are asking you. Remember, be interested and interesting in tandem.

If the person interviewing you tells you that they like their position because it gives them flexibility to spend weekends with their kids, your immediate follow-up to that could be, "That's great. How old are your children?" When they answer you, make one more statement or ask one more question. Show interest, but don't go down a rabbit hole. Here's the difference:

Acceptable

- "That's great. How old are they?"
- "Three and five."
- "That will certainly keep you busy. Those are fun ages."

Rabbit Hole

- "That's great. How old are they?"
- "Twelve and fifteen."
- "Teens, wow. Are they into sports?

- "My son plays football, and my daughter is in band."
- "I played football in high school. As a matter of fact, I was..."
- (Five minutes later, the interviewer will be looking at their watch.)

As you practice the interview process, ask the person helping you to be brutally honest. Ask them to look for rabbit holes, negative words, and filler words like "um" and "ah." When you go to a real interview, review these same things afterward. Keep a notebook in your car and jot down what went well, what you could improve upon, and anything interesting the interviewer told you that could be useful in your follow-up interview. Do this while it's fresh in your mind and before you pick up the phone to debrief your friend or significant other.

DRAW FROM YOUR EXPERIENCE

There are all sorts of experiences that make us interesting, experienced, and well-rounded, and these experiences don't have to come from work. When answering interview questions, drop hints about your life experiences and how they have helped you grow, learn, and develop valuable skills and qualities. Below are a few to get you thinking:

- Where you fit in the birth order, especially if you're the oldest, may tell an employer that you've grown up being responsible.
- Babysitting or being a camp counselor shows that others have trusted you with the people they value most—their children.
- Owning a pet shows that you're kind and likely to put others' needs first.

- Being a Boy Scout or Girl Scout, even if it was years ago, shows that you learned valuable life lessons and that you know how to work toward a goal.
- Taking care of an elderly parent or grandparent can demonstrate your loyalty and willingness to help others.
- Living with a disabled person in your home is a great lead-in to a conversation about gratitude or patience.
- Involvement in team sports or individual athletic pursuits can demonstrate teamwork, discipline, resilience, and goal-setting abilities.
- Participation in school clubs, student government, or community organizations can showcase leadership, organizational, and communication skills.
- Volunteer work or community service projects can reflect a sense of social responsibility, empathy, and a willingness to contribute to the greater good.
- Overcoming personal challenges or adversities, such as financial hardships, health issues, or difficult family situations, demonstrates perseverance, problem-solving skills, and emotional resilience.
- Entrepreneurial experiences, such as starting a small business or side hustle, can showcase initiative, creativity, and business acumen. This is also a great way to open a conversation on skills not necessarily listed on your résumé.
- Extensive travel or living abroad can indicate cultural awareness, adaptability, and a global mindset.
- Playing a musical instrument, writing, or playing chess can demonstrate passion, discipline, and a willingness to learn.

Draw on skills and qualities you've gained over the years to create an impression of yourself as well rounded. It's a good way for you to demonstrate how your unique background has prepared you for a role while also making you more memorable. People hire people, not résumés.

What to Wear

There are plenty of articles telling you what to wear, and Pinterest is full of pinnable outfits, but this is not a one-size-fits-all answer (pun intended). Even regional fashion may override some of the information given here. Let's face it: not many people in Hawaii need to wear black suits to work. As you read through this section, remember that there may be additional caveats and local observations that are essential. If you get the chance to see what other employees at that company are wearing, either through social media, website posts, or a trip to their parking lot at the beginning of the day, pick something similar.

Dress for the profession and the company. A construction superintendent should not show up in a three-piece suit, and someone wearing khakis will not come across as professional enough for the financial sector. Unless you're a college student applying for a casual on-campus job, you should never show up in jeans or flip-flops—even if you paid a fortune for them.

If you're applying for a creative position, such as the director of marketing, graphic artist, or special events coordinator, wear color and show off some tasteful fashion. Positions that call for a more analytical mind may call for black on the bottom and a solid color on top. Depending on the professional level of the position, a suit jacket may also be appropriate.

I once studied color psychology and have since used this in everything from design to business meetings. People relate to colors in unique ways, often subconsciously. If I have an important meeting with a large potential corporate client, I will often wear black slacks and a solid blouse that matches their logo's main color. Another excellent color trick is to mirror something specific about the person interviewing you.

If you know what university they graduated from, wear a blouse or tie in the color of their alma mater. Colors unify us in unspoken ways. We use certain colors for holidays and patriotism, and we even mourn in a specific color. Let what you wear subconsciously influence the person you're interviewing with.

Color-Code Your Influence

Red exudes power. Women can use red to leverage stature in a male-driven meeting. Women interviewing with other women may want to avoid red, as it can be seen as intimidating or confrontational. Men should avoid wearing red altogether during the interview process, as it may be seen as overbearing.

Blue signals trust because it represents sincerity and authenticity. Many hospitals and banks use blue in their logos because they know its power. Bright or deep blue works best for an interview outfit. Avoid pastels unless the position requires nurturing of some sort.

Orange is a mixture of red and yellow and combines happiness with confidence. This is a great color for creatives or if a position requires enthusiasm or encouragement. Also, if it's a color from the alma mater, by all means, wear it! If the color is from their alma mater's rival, avoid it completely.

Yellow is often associated with joy and brightness, but it's tricky. Too much of a good thing is not necessarily a good thing. Studies show that some people can be overwhelmed by this color, and even babies in yellow nurseries tend to cry more. This color is best used in small amounts.

Black is great if you're looking for formality or elegance. People who wear black can look mysterious, dangerous, or overly serious if it's not balanced with either white or another light color. A black suit with a contrasting shirt is a great bet for most interviews.

White is perhaps the safest color to wear during an interview. Obviously, not full white unless your job is to be the bride. White dress shirts and blouses symbolize honesty, purity, and a successful beginning. For women, be sure your underclothing is not showing through your white outfit.

Gray is the color of compromise, mixing the power of black with the safety and cleanliness of white. It also goes well with just about any accent color, which makes it versatile when dressing it up or dressing it down.

What to Bring

Now that you're confidently dressed, do you know what to bring? Always show up with two copies of your résumé (preferably on high-quality paper), a separate page of at least three references, and copies of any reference letters you may have collected from previous employers. You should also have copies of certifications, licenses, or other items of interest. Invest in a nice folder or portfolio to hold these items.

If you're being interviewed by someone who has written a book, bring a copy and ask for a signature. I have had a couple of candidates do this over the years, and I was always impressed that they did their homework. If you haven't read it yet, be honest. There is nothing worse than being put on the spot with a question like, "What was your favorite chapter?" or "What did you find the most helpful about the book?"

The Interview

Arrive five to ten minutes early, but never more than fifteen. When you walk in for the interview, smile and be friendly to everyone you meet. I often ask our receptionist to rank her first impression of the candidate before they come to the back of the office for the interview. Candidates who smile, shake hands, and clearly express who they are, why they're there, and make good eye contact get a high score. Any candidate who does not make a good first impression on our receptionist will most likely not make a good first impression on our patients. The receptionist or executive assistant has far more clout than you may want to believe. They are your first test, so be sure to pass it by leaving a great impression.

When you meet the person you'll be interviewing with, be sure to smile, shake their hand with a firm handshake, and follow their lead. The first thing you say should always be an expression of gratitude. A great example is, "Thank you for taking the time to interview me. I'm excited about this company and this position." Sit up tall but not so stiff that you look terrified. Breathe and smile. You've practiced this, you've done your homework, and you're prepared, so there is no need to be afraid or anxious. Just be your best, confident, likable you. The more confident you are in yourself, the more confident they will be in you.

Once the interview is nearing the end, it's your job to ask about next steps. Never assume that you'll be offered the job or that they intend to hire on the first interview. Toward the end of the conversation, assure them that you are interested in the position. If you haven't done so during the interview, ask about the hiring process. Breathe and smile. Gauge their reaction and match their enthusiasm level. If they seem serious, use serious words like, "I respect the interview process. Could you share the next steps with me?" If they're more casual, you can ask in a more relaxed fashion: "How long will you be taking to make your hiring decision?" No matter what their demeanor, you must always smile. Friendly questions you can end with include, "I enjoyed our time together. When would be a good time to follow up with you?" or "I can't wait to visit with you again. May I follow up with you in a day or two?"

Whatever you wear, dress intentionally. Whatever you speak, do so purposefully. Whatever you do, execute with purpose.

Impressive Impressions

The First Impression

Always be friendly to the receptionist and anyone else you come in contact with during the interview process.

When entering the interview room, make direct eye contact and offer a warm greeting to the interviewer. As you approach them, take a step forward with your left foot while extending your right hand for a handshake. Grip firmly but avoid an overly strong squeeze. Give one confident pump while introducing yourself clearly. Release the handshake smoothly and take a step back with your left foot to establish a comfortable distance between you and the interviewer. A well-executed handshake conveys confidence, professionalism, and respect, setting the tone for a positive interaction from the outset.

The Last Impression

As the interview concludes, be sure to push your chair back in neatly. Thank the interviewer for their time while making eye contact and shaking their hand again with the same firm, confident grip. Express your sincere interest in the role and enthusiasm for the opportunity. A simple statement such as, "I'm very excited about this position and believe my skills and experience are a match for this position" can reinforce your desire for the job. Be sure to leave with a genuine, friendly smile. The final impression can leave a lasting impact on the interviewer's perception of you. A warm, polished exit is just as important as a strong introduction in creating a positive and professional image.

"DILIGENT FOLLOW-UP AND FOLLOW-THROUGH WILL SET YOU APART FROM THE CROWD AND COMMUNICATE EXCELLENCE."

—John C. Maxwell, author and orator

CHAPTER 9

WHEN AND HOW TO FOLLOW UP

Perhaps the most nerve-racking part of the interview process is the moments or days afterward. Most interviewees will replay the interview details over and over in their heads in search of the positive or negative points. We tend to do this because the uncertainty of the future can seem unbearable. This chapter is dedicated to the follow-up process because having a plan will help combat post-interview anxiety and reduce unnecessary stress.

My mother used to tell me, "You can only control what you can control." This advice has served me well throughout my life. It will serve you well, too, as you navigate your job search. Putting effort into the things you can control and relinquishing the things you have no control over will help you stay sane and empower you in ways you could never have imagined.

It sounds counterintuitive that letting go of control will help you have more control. But you never had control over other people's thoughts and actions, and you never will. It's just a lie you've told yourself. Don't feel bad; you're not alone. Most stress, anxiety, and depression are rooted in that same lie. Some would argue that it's what keeps the pharmaceutical industry afloat. I would bet that 90 percent or more of the other candidates are fretting over these things they can't control. Knowing you can't control what the potential employer is going to do and accepting that will put you one step ahead.

Other candidates may be running their interview on a continuous thought loop and in their heads saying, "I bet they won't call," or "They probably thought that answer was stupid." Unlike them, your focus should instead be on what you can control. Your thoughts should sound more like, "I did my best, and now it's time to follow up as planned," or "What did I learn from that interview to help me with my follow-up strategy?"

There is no one-size-fits-all solution for follow-up. Following up with each company and even after each interview within the same company will be handled differently. Your words and actions should be appropriate and reflect the experience.

Universal Dos and Don'ts for Following Up

Do be sure to proofread any written form of follow-up before you send it.

Do keep your tone professional but not impersonal, pleasant but not overly friendly.

Do address the person as they've asked to be addressed. If you called them Karen in the interview, don't follow up with Ms. Smith, and vice versa.

Do mention something specific about the interview you liked. For example: "Thank you for taking me on a tour. I was very impressed with the facility."

Do send a thank-you email or letter the same day.

Don't follow up after business hours. Nobody wants to be emailed or texted during dinner or after they have gone to bed.

Don't use abbreviations or slang in your message. ("TY" does *not* equal "thank you.")

Don't use emojis when texting or emailing.

Don't become a stalker. One thank-you after the interview and one follow-up after that is sufficient unless they specifically ask you to reach out again later.

Don't ever use language that assumes you have the job before it's offered. Instead of "When you hire me for this position...," use "If I'm offered this position...."

The detective skills you developed previously will also help you make your follow-up plan. It's a natural tendency to assume what people want. We often make assumptions by asking ourselves, "What would I want?" It's a fair question, but it's the wrong one. What we want is rarely the same as what others want. So instead, ask yourself, "What did I learn about the interviewer's style? How would they like me to follow up with them?" If you asked during the interview, good for you! If you didn't ask them directly, then use your context clues.

Over the years, I have received letters, texts, emails, and even a plant after an interview. Which one was best? I can't answer that objectively because each situation was different. A physician I interviewed after hours via phone later sent me a text thanking me for the conversation. That was not only fine, but it was also appropriate. A nurse I interviewed in the office texted me a week later on my cell at 6:30 p.m. That was not appropriate. First, I did not give her my cell; she obtained it from our receptionist. Second, she texted after hours. It had nothing to do with the professional rank or class of the candidate; it had everything to do with respect and boundaries.

A written letter can be a nice touch, but it may not be your best option, depending on the hiring time frame. The fine linen paper, the perfect spacing, and the carefully chosen words will have little impact if your letter is received the day after the company makes its decision. If the position has a long lead time and the company has taken a more formal approach to the interview process, then a professional, mailed letter may be the right approach.

Dropping off a small gift or sending a plant is certainly not appropriate after a first interview, but it may be a nice touch after the second or third. If a company flies you in for an interview and spends hours with you, consider that more than a first date, and send a small token of appreciation within three days.

In most cases, a friendly email will suffice following the first interview. The email should be short and sweet. Address them by name, write one sentence of gratitude for their time, mention something you liked about the interview in the next sentence or two, then end it on a positive note. Always end with how much you look forward to speaking with them again.

After your follow-up, you will either get a reply or you won't. Don't read anything into either of these options. A cordial reply does not mean you have the job (unless they say so), and silence does not mean you don't. You don't know what you don't know, and until you have facts that support their decision either way, don't second-guess it.

The timing of the second follow-up depends on their urgency, not yours. During the interview, you should have gathered clues about how soon they plan to fill the position. Your response should be geared to match their goals. If they said, "We are looking to hire in the next couple weeks," then your second follow-up should be in five to seven days. On the contrary, if they desire to hire within the next six months, you could schedule your second follow-up in a couple of weeks to a month and possibly reach out one more time a month later based on their previous response.

While each company and interviewer have different expectations, below is an example of a successful follow-up that was memorable for me and led to a job offer for this candidate.

Me (call via cell phone): "I received your résumé from Shelly, and I may have a position you'd be interested in. Do you have time for a conversation?"

Candice: "I am actually not available right now, but I will be from noon to 2:30 p.m. or after 4 p.m. today. Would that work for you?" (Note: it's okay to say no if you offer an alternative time.)

I spoke to Candice for quite some time and determined that a face-to-face meeting would be best. Since this was for a professional organization, not my office, I invited her to attend that organization's 7:00 a.m. meeting the following morning. She arrived early and professionally dressed and was able to meet members of the organization and visit with the executive board. Her conversations proved that she had done her research. She was more interested than interesting, and her smile and handshakes exuded confidence. Before leaving at 8:30 a.m., she was sure to say "Good-bye" and "Thank you" to each member of the board, which she had identified previously through the website.

Candice (text to my cell phone at 9:48 a.m.): "This is Candice. I want to take the time to thank you for the opportunity to apply for the administration position with (named the organization). You guided and led me through the whole process, which was much appreciated. You are so impressive and empowering on the phone and even more so in person. I know in all confidence that I could do an efficient, organized, and personalized job with good energy for (named the organization). Thank you for inviting me to be a part of it this morning. It was an honor to meet you in person, and I look forward to hearing the next steps. Here's to you writing your best book ever and an incredibly successful year."

Imagine for a moment that you're Candice, who sent that text, and five hours later, you still haven't heard back. I wasn't ignoring her; I was simply in back-to-back meetings. Finally, at 3:35 p.m., I responded.

Luckily, she had the patience to wait for my reply. An additional text would have been inappropriate. It would have screamed desperation and impatience. Instead, her ability to sit and wait for a reply gave me clues. If she could respect my time, she would most likely respect other board members and their time.

Me (via text): Such kind words, thank you. Sorry for the late reply! I have been running all day! I'll call you in a bit.

Candice: I look forward to talking with you.

At 5:00 p.m., I called to let her know she was the chosen candidate. During that call, she asked specific questions about the next steps and expressed her gratitude. Truth be told, if the organization didn't hire her, I would have hired her at our medical practice. Some candidates have "it," and she certainly had "it."

At that same meeting, there was another candidate who was also strong. The other candidate did everything right, and she also arrived early and sent a follow-up text. Either candidate could have done the job and done it well. Candice was just the most suited for the position. It was the little things that pushed Candice into the position of front-runner and landed her the position. Just like her, it's the little things that will make you the *most* qualified candidate in a room full of qualified candidates.

"LET US NEVER NEGOTIATE OUT OF FEAR. BUT LET US NEVER FEAR TO NEGOTIATE."

—John F. Kennedy, thirty-fifth US president

CHAPTER 10

DECIDING TO ACCEPT OR NEGOTIATE

Negotiating a salary is invigorating for some, nerve-racking for others, and a small percentage will never know what it feels like. That's because, according to a study reported by Salary.com, 37 percent of employees negotiate salaries often, and 18 percent have never negotiated a salary before. What holds us back from asking a question? Fear. What is the best antidote to fear? Once again, the answer is preparation. This chapter is designed to give you the tools you need as you decide if an offer is worthy of acceptance or if there is justification for some negotiation. While it's impossible to predict every situation, many companies welcome or even expect some negotiation.

In 2021, XpertHR conducted a recruiting and hiring survey, and 324 organizations responded on topics related to their flexibility of total compensation packages. Of those respondents, 90 percent said they would be open to negotiating the base salary for at least some positions. When asked about bonuses, 42 percent said they were open to negotiation. The percentage dropped to 32 percent when asked about their willingness to negotiate benefits. Some of the decrease in flexibility when it came to benefits and bonuses may have been related to legalities, company policy, or even the headache of increased paper-work on behalf of human resources. These statistics prove the importance of negotiating the base salary before attempting to negotiate anything else.

As you read through the next few pages, understand that not every job or salary is negotiable. Many factors come into play. Some of these factors include the economy, the unemployment rate, labor force availability for the specific profession or skill set needed, and the company's financial flexibility. Getting a particular salary at one company, in one location, for a specific shift does not mean the same offer would apply elsewhere. The same is true for internet searches that result in misleading salary expectations. Just because you read it somewhere doesn't mean it's factual, realistic, or attainable.

Most people think of negotiation as getting more money, particularly more money than their last job paid. There are so many more factors than just salary. This is where thinking more like a chess player who strategizes every move works to your benefit. Base salary is important, but so is job title, growth opportunity, continuing education, and time off. Remember to see your salary as simply part of the compensation package. As you build your package, think strategically about what you want to accomplish. Will your new job title help you climb the corporate ladder in the future? Does the extra week off allow you more time to vacation or visit loved ones?

The negotiation process begins *long* before you get to the in-person interview. Just like researching potential future employers, there is a process for researching compensation. Keep in mind that the PEP gave you the opportunity to research and record facts specific to a specific company. When completing the Compensation Reference Model (CRM) found in this chapter, the information will be from outside sources. It may or may not apply specifically to the specific company or job for which you are applying. Yet it is tremendously valuable because it helps justify a particular ask in the negotiation.

At this point, you may be sighing and wondering why so much work must go into all this. Nothing worth getting is easy. If this process helps you successfully negotiate a higher compensation package, then the work will be worth it. If you do the exercise and don't successfully negotiate a higher compensation package, at least you will be making an informed decision to accept or decline the offer. Nobody likes second-guessing their decision, and peace of mind is still of value. Either way, this is a win-win. As always, you can find a downloadable version of the CRM on StopWhiningStartWorking.com.

CRM

This model can help determine a person's professional value, the current job market, if an offer is fair and competitive, and the potential added value or devalue of a job offer. Information gathered may be used to justify a higher compensation request or determine if an offer presented is of value.

Professional value: First start with what you, the potential employee, bring to the table. This has nothing to do with what you think you can do, but everything to do with facts. Focus on anything you can prove or use a solid reference to support your claim.

Education level/degrees:_____

_____

Relevance of such degree or field of study to this position:

_____

_____

Internships, externships, or continued education:

_____

_____

Professional accolades or awards:_____

_____

_____

Professional bragging rights (For example, "Grew revenue by 110 percent over the course of a year."):

_____

_____

The current job market: These things are out of your control. They can work in your favor or against you, but either way, you need to know what they are. This is where only current statistics matter. If you're looking at data that's a few years old, it may be completely obsolete. Dig deep, do your research, and put in the time required to paint an accurate picture of the current job market for this position. Some helpful websites for research purposes include www.BLS.gov, www.Salary.com, www.Statista.com, and local and state labor statistic websites.

Current unemployment rate:_____

_____

What's affecting the current unemployment rate? Does it affect this particular company or this type of position?

_____

Number of recent graduates with the same degree required for this position:_____

How common or rare is the required experience?

_____

Average starting salary for this position:_____

_____

Average salary listed on other job postings for the same type of position in the same demographic area (Check Indeed, Monster, ZipRecruiter, and other sites.):_____

_____

Additional value or devalue: This may be the most important yet most ignored piece of the puzzle. The answers here will help identify future growth or uncertainty within the company. Start with the company's website, news sites, LinkedIn, and even sites like www.Glassdoor.com, www.Comparably.com, or other company feedback sites.

Company's years in business:_____

If public, how does the company rank in liquidity, solvency, profitability, and operating efficiency?

_____

List any news about the company that is either good or bad:

_____

_____

How do past employees describe their experience with the company?

_____

Is there evidence that the company promotes from within? (Use LinkedIn and other sources for research.)

_____

Do people stay with the company for more than three years? (Use LinkedIn and other sources for research.)

_____

What is the average rating on the company's Google reviews? What are people saying?

_____

_____

Is there any evidence that this company or the industry will go bankrupt or become obsolete in the next five years?

_____

If this is a start-up company, is it well-funded? If so, by whom?

_____

Does this company offer stock options or other additional benefits that may yield a high return? If so, what?

_____

The CRM provides the much-needed data to determine whether a job offer is right for you, sometimes before the interview. A company that sounded good in the beginning may not look good after a more careful review of its future. Nobody wants to go down with a sinking ship. Other times, the CRM will provide more excitement about a potential employer because it offers long-term growth opportunities and job security.

If you're offered a position and want to negotiate, be sure to negotiate from a position of power. Because you've done your homework, you know your strengths, your competition, the market, and some vital information about the company. This doesn't mean you show up as a know-it-all. Instead, you present yourself as a humble yet well-informed candidate who has something to offer. You are seeking compensation that is fair to both parties.

Most career coaches will tell you that countering a base salary is something a company may expect and that your counter can be in the range of 10 to 20 percent above their starting point. This doesn't mean they will go as high as 20 percent, but it does give them room to counter back. Going above 20 percent is risky for many reasons. The employer may think you are not serious about their offer and may assume you will be looking to make a higher salary elsewhere shortly after they hire you. If the company offers something that is more than 20 percent below market and you don't see other benefits that make up the difference, you may politely decline. Remember the nevers: *never* insult and *never* burn a bridge because you *never* know when that person will be with a different company in the future.

Being prepared for a negotiation will give you the confidence you need as you enter into this phase of the interview process. Know what your acceptable range is, the benefits that will sweeten the deal for you, and the threshold of which you are willing to walk away from the offer. Be bold, be empowered, and always be polite and humble.

How *Not* to Negotiate

The following is a list of tactics that should never enter the negotiation conversation. While you may find them comical, someone has said these things before. It goes without saying, but *no* they did not work, and in some cases, the job offer was completely rescinded.

- I need a higher offer because I have loads of credit card debt.

- I deserve higher pay because I will be driving farther to get here than my last job.

- You must pay me more because I am currently making that amount.

- Your CEO makes millions of dollars, and I think you should pay people like me more than what you're offering.

- I know you advertised that you need someone 8:00 a.m. to 5:00 p.m., but I have other commitments. Can I leave for a few hours in the middle of the day or work part-time?

- Here's a list of salaries from Salary.com, and it shows your offer is too low.

- I need to make more because my spouse stays home.

- You should pay me more because I have a degree that has nothing to do with this job, but I worked hard for it.

How *to* Negotiate

- Discuss the relevant benefits you bring to the company. (You listed these on your CRM.)

- I see you are offering ____. I believe I can bring value to your company, and my experience with ____ makes me a strong candidate. I'd like to discuss a salary of (10 to 20 percent above offer).

- Would you be willing to offer ____ after ninety days if I can prove to you that I am proficient in ____?

- I understand that your base salary is set. Could we create a bonus structure tied to performance or growth key performance indicators (KPIs)?

Once you've settled on a base salary that both parties are comfortable with, review the benefits. Some benefits may not be negotiable, while others, such as yearly executive physical examinations, paid parking, tuition reimbursement, continuing education, and increased paid time off, may be. As you negotiate these additional benefits, know that it must make sense for the company's bottom line. Sometimes, the company may need to weigh whether they can afford to extend the benefit you're asking for to everyone else. If the answer is no, they will most likely decline or seek legal counsel to ensure they aren't breaking any laws by singling the benefit out.

How *to* Negotiate Around Benefits

- Wellness is important to me and will make me a stronger employee for your company. Do you offer additional wellness benefits, or can we negotiate these into the employment agreement?
- I see the parking fees are not part of the benefits offered. Is there a way to include them or split them?
- I understand that your benefits are nonnegotiable. Since the cost of your healthcare insurance is higher than I expected, can we negotiate a higher base salary?

Remember that negotiation is an art. You aren't telling them what to do or asking them to agree with everything you say. The goal is to find a middle ground that has both people walking away feeling good about the experience. Stay positive, be friendly, and be thankful for any give on their end. How well you negotiate will be remembered and will set the tone for mutual respect.

"THE GREATEST ASSET OF A COMPANY IS ITS PEOPLE."

—Jorge Paulo Lemann, cofounder, Banco Garantia

CHAPTER 11

HOW TO BECOME THE STAR EMPLOYEE

Society will tell you we shouldn't have favorites, but that goes against the science of human nature. Preferences are part of how we make decisions about everything from the flavor of ice cream we eat, the clothes we wear, the people we hire, and the employees we managers and business owners choose to promote. Having been a middle manager, a small business owner, and now the CEO of a multimillion-dollar company, I can assure you of one thing: you cannot whine yourself to the top.

There are many myths surrounding what makes a good employee a star employee. Being early or on time, dressing well, and having incredible skills are all important, but these are basic expectations every employee should live up to. I once had a medical assistant who was never late and was incredibly skilled at drawing blood, giving shots, and charting. In her eyes, she was a star employee, and she even verbalized what a great employee she was, not just to me but to others at work. Although she was a good employee, I did not agree with her self-assessment that she was a "star"—and neither did her coworkers. As I like to say, "She was unaware that she was unaware."

This employee had the basics down but didn't take the initiative. She was great at carrying out a task as asked, but she didn't contribute to new ideas or new processes that could have made everyone's workload, including hers, easier. She was also so busy with her nose to the grindstone, trying to get her own tasks done efficiently, that she rarely took the time to offer others help or a smile or to build working relationships. She was not a star. But she could have been.

My experience with this employee is not an uncommon one. Most businesses have employees who are much like her. I spend a great deal of time with other CEOs and business owners, and I've noticed that there are employee "types" who seem to work at almost all organizations. In addition to the "good enough" employee, there is the "better than everyone else" employee. This is the person who spends their workday just waiting for someone to break the rules, make a mistake, or not live up to their standards. They catalog offenses all day, every day. They then use these errors or omissions to fuel their argument about why they are the obvious choice for the next promotion, a raise, or, at the very least, favor with the boss. It's fair to say that nobody likes a "better than everyone else" type, not the coworkers and especially not the management. Even if they garner favor with management for a short period of time, they look foolish when they make a mistake, and inevitably, they will make a mistake. And as karma would have it, the mistake they make will usually be a big one.

Many businesses have employees with bona fide star potential. A few of those employees will reach that potential if they are willing to learn, grow, and balance humility with drive. The fact that you're reading this chapter will give you the edge because you're starting to recognize what it takes to become invaluable to your employer. In this chapter, you'll learn the basic expectations and how to go above and beyond those so your contribution is valuable and your employment is tenable.

There will be many things to add to your to-do list as you strive to improve. In addition, there are things you'll need to remove. There are words to say and words not to say, things to do and things not to do, ways to act and ways not to act. All the while, you should never forget that the number one rule is to be authentic because when rising to the top, there is no room for fake or disingenuous attributes. You must have the desire to do better and be better. As you keep it real, remember that the decision for excellence is not temporary. Excellence comes with continuous improvement and constant self-examination, both of which can't happen unless you are also self-aware. To increase your chances for employment and advancement, pay attention to what you say, your true motives, how you act and react, and how others react to and interact with you. As you examine these, do it with an honest heart, never playing the victim, as you look for ways to grow and improve.

Stardom begins at the interview and continues throughout employment. In Tarki's book, *Evidence-Based Recruiting: How to Build a Company of Star Performers Through Systematic and Repeatable Hiring Practices,* he teaches hiring teams what to look for in candidates so they can hire the right person. You want to be that right person. Even if you don't have experience within the industry you are applying to, you can still stand out as having star potential by showing initiative. Do what Tarki preaches by not just saying you have an interest but by showing it. Learn industry-specific language by reading blogs or industry-specific magazines, or better yet, volunteer to gain some much-needed experience. Tarki's advice is great for the interview process and continues to be important even after you land the job.

Initiative may be your most important trait, so consider it a superpower. Like all superpowers, yours must be managed and perfected because, left untamed, they could work against you. Nobody likes a new employee who comes in with too many ideas and suggests changes before they have a clear understanding of the company's processes. The employees who get involved and take time to learn the ins and outs of the business, the processes, and the why behind the processes are the ones best suited to make suggestions. Their suggestions also have the best chance of being implemented because they will have been well thought out. As Stephen R. Covey says, "Seek first to understand, then to be understood." This is the fifth habit in his book *The 7 Habits of Highly Effective People.* If you haven't already read this book, make it the next book you read. It was one of the first leadership books I ever read, and decades later, I'm still living by those seven habits.

As you grow and flex your leadership muscle, remember that misguided or premature initiative by a new employee can backfire and reflect poorly on your character. I often ask new employees to "stay in their lane" until they have mastered the course. Golfers know this concept well. Just because a golfer knows the game of golf and may be a good player, it doesn't make them an expert on every course. This takes understanding the course, getting a feel for it, and even soliciting tips from those who've played it before. Every new employer is like a new golf course. Even if you think the path or the job is easy, there are hidden sand traps everywhere, which can be political, historical, or interpersonal.

Political Sand Traps

Let's say Sam takes the position of new area sales director for a regional magazine. He's been in sales before but has never sold in the publishing industry. Within a few weeks of being hired, he directs his sales team to reach out to five oil and gas companies to secure advertising in the magazine. They are mildly successful and sell roughly $10,000 in ad space. Imagine his surprise when their long-time back cover advertiser pulls their business.

Unbeknownst to Sam, that back cover advertiser who spent $15,000 per month and has done so for the last three years has put his company through a major green energy initiative. Sam has fallen into a political sand trap. This cost him his relationship with that major advertiser and put his sales team at a disadvantage because now they have to manage multiple accounts that don't even add up to the monthly amount they were getting from one advertiser.

Historical Sand Traps

These sand traps can be the trickiest because unlike political sand traps, these take time to surface and rarely come up in casual conversation. All companies, even the most successful ones, come with bad decisions and experiences. These missteps have shaped the company's current processes and have left the leaders snakebitten. Let's say Jane takes a new position at the bank. Her goal is to find a path to leadership. She's with the company about a week before she goes to her boss with a list of management courses she's researched and wants to take. In addition, she wants the bank to pay for her courses. Jane assumes her idea will be met with equal enthusiasm; after all, she's taken the initiative to better herself.

What Jane didn't know is that the bank employee she replaced was always taking time off, which added to everyone's workload. Her supervisor was less than thrilled when Jane, within one week of being hired, was already researching things to do other than what she was hired for. Knowing and understanding historical context will help you find the right time and way to approach your leadership goals. Remember, context is important. Ask questions and get to know the context in which you were hired.

Interpersonal Sand Traps

It takes time to understand the dynamics within a company, but interpersonal relationships can be understood if you're willing to take the time to observe. Failure to do so may land you in the interpersonal sand trap. John came to his new company with many great ideas. He was so excited that he took one of his ideas straight to the owner, bypassing the CEO. Then, when approaching the CEO, he led with the news that the owner loved the idea and felt the company should move forward. (Wasn't it the *Lost in Space* show that coined the term "Danger, danger, Will Robinson"?)

John's CEO thought the concept was worthy of discussion, but he could see the idea as presented wouldn't work. If John had gone through the chain of command, he could have fleshed out the idea and presented a workable model. To make matters worse, the owner was under the assumption that John had already discussed the idea with the CEO and was shocked to find out he hadn't. Even if John's idea in some form becomes implemented, he has fallen into the inter-personal sand trap. In doing so, he lost some trust from the CEO and possibly some from the owner, who will be reluctant to hear him out in the future. While this example has to do with the chain of command, many interpersonal issues are much less obvious.

The best way to avoid all types of sand traps is to be an observer. Talk less, listen more, and be curious. Engage in work social events but do so from an observer's standpoint. Pay attention to the relationships employees have with each other, their customers, and the leadership. As you take mental notes, do so without prejudice or judgment. Your mission is simply a fact-finding one. The information you gather will help you learn how and where you fit in, the company's and other employees' needs, and the hot buttons you should avoid.

Learning the ins and outs of the new business is vital to your future success. Remember that everything stable starts with a good foun-dation. That's why the ten attributes listed below are nonnegotiable. Perfect yourself and your performance first. Then, use the information you gathered about the company and the company dynamics as the framework for presenting your ideas and suggestions.

10 Ps to Being a Star Employee

Be:

- [ ] **Punctual.** This means being five minutes early and showing up dressed and ready.
- [ ] **Prepared.** Show up in the right mindset. Have your to-do list ready and a plan of attack prepared.
- [ ] **Positive.** Look for the good in everything you do and in everyone you see.
- [ ] **Predictable.** People who are predictable (in a good way) earn trust faster. Show your supervisor you're consistent and dependable in all that you do.
- [ ] **Polished.** Look nice, act nice, and keep a nice and neat work area. People who are polished come across as much more trustworthy and capable.
- [ ] **Passionate.** Be passionate about something. Passion is what makes people interesting. When expressing your passion, remember that it's your passion and may not be everyone else's favorite topic. Be passionate but never pushy.
- [ ] **Peaceful.** Individuals who are peaceful naturally attract others to them, while those who thrive on chaos repel those around them. Be peaceful, which is different from passive. Peaceful people are pleasant to work with because they care and never stir up drama.
- [ ] **Practical.** Look for ideas that work in the real world, not just on paper or in theory. Be open to others fleshing out your ideas without becoming defensive.
- [ ] **Proactive.** Always look to be part of the solution rather than part of the problem. Avoid the echo chamber of complaints and be the one who steps up.

☐ **Professional.** Act the part. Even if you naturally tend to be a jokester, lazy, or use choice words—don't do it at work. Professionalism breeds respect.

The ten "P" words above are not an all-inclusive list. Think of other ways you can become a star within your company or your industry.

You may have noticed that the word "perfect" is not listed. There is not a single perfect employee. Even the brightest of stars flicker now and then. Take the pressure off yourself to be perfect. Focus on what you can do and what you should do. If you focus your efforts on self-improvement, you'll be moving in the right direction.

Star employees take time to understand the goals of the company. Ask questions. Be curious. Look for ways that your skill set or interests may align with their goals, but don't disclose them until you have a plan that makes sense. Great ideas that are wasted with bad timing are a tragedy, but presenting a great idea at the right time can be career-changing.

For example, Brandon just took a job with an auto parts chain. He had years of experience in the auto industry and was very talented at mechanics. On the side, Brandon also had a modest number of social media followers and enjoyed making videos. When he learned that the company's goals were to engage their customers with the hopes of doubling their sales for the coming year, he took time to write a proposal, considering what he had learned about the company culture. He asked his immediate supervisor for feedback and then asked permission to present the proposal formally to him and the owner. His supervisor felt included and respected and was excited to bring the idea up the chain. Within three months, Brandon was spending half his time making "how-to" videos for their consumers. He featured some of their most profitable products, and by the end of the year, he had a new title, a pay raise, and an expanded online following. The company also benefited from record sales, which exceeded their goal. The right idea presented at the right time was career-changing.

Many people have the potential to be a star within their company, industry, or profession. I believe you have what it takes to earn that star title. Scientifically speaking, stars are self-luminous by nature, meaning they radiate their own heat and light energy. That's what gives them their glow, which can be seen from light-years away. You, too, can shine bright and become a star simply by putting forth effort, positive energy, and deliberate actions.

"LEADERS ARE RESPONSIBLE FOR CREATING AN ENVIRONMENT IN WHICH PEOPLE FEEL THEY CAN BE THEIR BEST."

—Simon Sinek, author and inspirational speaker

CHAPTER 12

THE LEADER WITHIN YOU

Every year, thousands of books are published on the topic of leadership. This means there's a large market for these books. People are searching for how to be a leader, or how to be a better leader, because they know there's value in leadership qualities. It's true. Employees exhibiting these qualities have a greater chance of being promoted, increasing their income, and ultimately creating their own success stories. I believe everyone has a secret leader hidden inside of them who desires to be set free, but not everyone will do the work to get it out. Hidden leaders get frustrated and stall, but liberated leaders get excited and produce incredible results.

If we look at the evolution of leadership over the years, some things have stayed the same, while others have emerged. For example, leaders need to be able to make tough decisions, have self-discipline, laser focus, and a vision for the future. These attributes allow them to successfully run a company, an organization, and even their own life. Terms like "servant leader" and "people manager" have been used to describe even the highest level of leadership within a company. I was recently told that CEO no longer stands for "chief executive officer" but rather "chief employee officer" because a company without focused and dedicated employees will not succeed in the test of time. Great leaders aren't dictators or tyrants, or self-absorbed. Instead, they are engaging and respectful yet firm.

Some people subscribe to the idea that leaders are born. I'm not of that mindset. Nobody is born engaging, respectful, or knowing how to set boundaries. These are learned attributes that come with experience and knowledge. While being naturally charismatic and extroverted may help make the road to leadership easier, I've met many great introverted leaders who had to sharpen their people skills as they grew in their careers. If you struggle with communication, likability, decision-making, or any other leadership skill, these are the areas you should focus on, not shy away from. True leaders aren't dictators; they lead others to do better and be better. If you're going to become a leader, then you must learn how to relate to the leaders you admire.

"GET AROUND PEOPLE WHO HAVE SOMETHING OF VALUE TO SHARE WITH YOU. THEIR IMPACT WILL CONTINUE TO HAVE A TREMENDOUSLY ENRICHING EFFECT ON YOUR LIFE."
—Les Brown

The only way to cultivate experience is to put yourself in the position of gaining it. There are many ways to gather leadership skills in and out of the work environment. Some of the greatest skills I've learned came from working within the community and volunteering for nonprofit organizations. There are always ways to get involved, and I encourage you to step outside of your comfort zone, enter a room full of strangers, and learn how to strive toward a common goal. Don't know where to start? The end of this chapter has a list of quick and easy ways to connect.

A few decades ago, I joined a local newcomer's club of women within my community. I started as a member and spent a year or two getting to know the other women in the group. When it came time to nominate a new board of directors, a fellow member encouraged me to run. To my surprise, I was elected. I remember my first meeting because I had never been to a board meeting before, and it was a bit overwhelming. By being an avid observer, taking notes, and later looking up terms like "P&L" and "point of order," I soon became comfortable and took a more active role in the discussion and decisions. Now, I not only understand how an organization works from the top down, but I'm also currently the board president of an executive association in one of America's largest cities. Every leader starts somewhere.

Leadership is a skill that needs to be honed. Educate yourself, and then practice, practice, practice. Start with reading books on leadership, listening to podcasts on the topic, and observing leaders you respect. As you do this, take notes. What attributes does this leader have? How do they approach people, talk to them, or get them to come to a consensus? As you listen to podcasts, read books, and shadow leaders, look for nuggets you can apply to your own life. Ask yourself, "What did I learn that I can apply today, this week?" Always be learning with the mindset of applying what you learned. Then, take it a step further. Journal what you learned, how you applied it, and if it worked. If you would have done something differently, write that down, too. Over time, this reflection will help you develop your own specific style of leadership.

Understanding who and what shaped your view of leadership will also be insightful. Take a moment to answer the following questions.

Who Shaped My View of Leadership?

1. Think back to the first person you ever saw as having authority in your life. How did they make you feel? In what aspect did they lead you and shape your decisions?

    _____

    _____

    _____

2. Reflect on a negative experience you had with someone in a position of authority. What did they do that made this a bad experience for you? What attributes did they have that you want to avoid in your own leadership style?

_____

_____

3. Did you have a favorite coach, teacher, or mentor growing up? What made them special? In what ways did they shape the person you are today?

_____

_____

4. Who has been your favorite boss? What did they do right? What could they have improved on?

_____

_____

My Leadership Aspirations

After reviewing your answers above, list the dos and don'ts that you want for your leadership style based on what you learned from past experience.

Leadership dos:

_____

_____

Leadership don'ts:

_____

_____

Take Action

It's time to get started on your journey. Look at the following recommendations of books to read and podcasts to listen to. You don't have to do them all, and you certainly don't need to do them all at one time. I try to read one book and listen to one podcast at a time, before moving on to the next one. The goal is not to check the box or see how many you can get through in the shortest time. Even if some of these books feel over your head or above where you currently are in your leadership journey, it's best to study where you want to be. As you read and listen, you'll also better understand the leaders around you. The goal is to learn, to absorb, and to evolve. Evolution takes time.

Books

- *The 7 Habits of Highly Effective People* by Stephen R. Covey
- *Dare to Lead* by Brené Brown
- *The 21 Irrefutable Laws of Leadership* by John C. Maxwell
- *Leadership and Self-Deception* by The Arbinger Institute
- *Lead Yourself First* by Raymond M. Kethledge and Michael S. Erwin
- *Unlocking Potential* by Michael Simpson
- *Leaders Eat Last* by Simon Sinek
- *How to Win Friends and Influence People* by Dale Carnegie
- *Extreme Ownership* by Jocko Willink and Leif Babin
- *Awaken the Giant Within* by Tony Robbins
- *Spark* by Angie Morgan, Courtney Lynch, and Sean Lynch
- *EntreLeadership* by Dave Ramsey
- *The Five Dysfunctions of a Team* by Patrick Lencioni
- *The Culture Code* by Daniel Coyle
- *Multipliers* by Liz Wiseman

- *The One Minute Manager* by Ken Blanchard and Spencer Johnson
- *The Myth of the Strong Leader* by Archie Brown

Podcasts

- *Inspiring Leadership* hosted by Jonathan Bowman-Perks
- *The Frame of Mind Coaching Podcast* hosted by Kim Ades and Ferne Kotlyar
- *The Tony Robbins Podcast* hosted by Tony Robbins and Sage Robbins
- *Lead to Succeed* hosted by Naphtali Hoff
- *Ask a CEO* hosted by Greg Demetriou
- *EntreLeadership* hosted by Dave Ramsey
- *The Tim Ferriss Show* hosted by Tim Ferriss

Short on time? Check out the Headway app. This great tool allows you to pick what you want to learn more about and then gives you a library of resources to choose from. The key points of each resource are presented succinctly. The best part is that you can either read them, listen to them, or do both. It's a great way to laser-focus your reading list and consume information quickly and effectively.

Get Connected within Your Community

- Kiwanis International: www.Kiwanis.org
- Rotary International: www.Rotary.org
- The chamber of commerce in your city
- Local church groups
- Local community center events
- The arts council within your community

University and college clubs (for students and mentors)

- Want to find more opportunities to connect within your community? Try these useful sites:
- www.MeetUp.com
- www.DownToMeet.com
- www.SucceedSocially.com

The most important part about being a good leader is being disciplined enough to lead yourself first. These tools will help you jump-start your ability to lead your own life. Studying the habits of leaders, not just in their work lives but also in their personal lives, will give you enormous insight into the realities of leadership. Look for patterns or common traits through reading, listening, and observing. You'll find that no matter what field of work leaders are in, they share commonalities. Adapt those same patterns and traits into your own life.

If you journal your progress and reflect on how your life is evolving, you'll be able to recognize change, identify what's working and not working, and how people are responding to your efforts. Adapt those traits in your own life and emulate leadership qualities in all that you do and in all that you say. Sooner rather than later, the leader within you will emerge. Imagine that I'm reading your journal and cheering you along on your progress. I believe in you, and deep down, you believe in yourself. You have a leader inside of you, so cheer that leader on, speak words of encouragement on the inside, and celebrate the small wins. Sometime soon, you will look back in amazement at all you have accomplished.

"IF WE WANT TO FEEL AN UNDYING PASSION FOR OUR WORK, IF WE WANT TO FEEL WE ARE CONTRIBUTING TO SOMETHING BIGGER THAN OURSELVES, WE ALL NEED TO KNOW OUR WHY."

—Simon Sinek, author of *Find Your Why: A Practical Guide for Discovering Purpose for You and Your Team*

CHAPTER 13

LET YOUR WHY DRIVE YOUR SUCCESS

Have you ever stopped to think about why you do the things you do? Often, we're on autopilot as we move from one task to the next. This is how we can drive from one location to another or down a familiar route and barely remember the trip. If we're not careful, our career can feel like that familiar route as we go from day to day, not paying any attention to where we want to be someday. Without a good sense of direction, a strategic plan to follow, and a good WHY driving your actions, someday will arrive, and you'll find yourself disappointed and perhaps shocked you didn't accomplish more. In this situation, it may be easy to blame others, but they are not in charge of your success; you are. Discovering your WHY is like filling up your future with rocket fuel and then turning on the GPS. You'll get things done faster and move in the right direction.

Everyone's WHY is different, as is how we discover our WHY. The person who came from poverty or uneducated parents may have a strong desire to make a better future for themselves and their children. Their WHY is financially driven because they desire stability and assurance. Someone else may have been told they would never make it as a manager; therefore, their goal is to prove that narrative false and instead prove themselves worthy. And yet another person may want to own their own company someday, so their WHY is based on gaining experience and having exposure to strong mentors in an effort to understand what success looks like and replicate it. Regardless of the individual reason, it's easy to see how having a strong WHY drives success.

Your WHY = Your Drive = Your Continued Success

Janet was good at many things. Her ability to run numbers and calculate financials was impressive—so much so that she worked her way up to VP of accounting at a large corporation. She had great benefits and competitive pay, but she worked long hours and often had to work weekends. In five years, she found herself burned out and looking for a different employer. She interviewed at multiple companies, but nothing sparked her interest. Since Janet had twenty-one days of unused paid time off, she took ten days of vacation to clear her head.

Janet, like so many of us, rarely afforded herself downtime, but it's in this downtime that our WHY shows up. Sometimes, it appears as a small whisper, while other times, it's like a hard slap in the face. Be open to both and be ready. We'll follow Janet's progress in this chapter.

WHY

W What speaks to the core of who I am or who I want to be?

H How do I get there? What's my strategic plan?

Y Yes, I can! (And you've got to believe it.)

What speaks to the core of who I am or who I want to be?

This is the deep dive, the hard question that can't be answered on a whim. If your answer today is different from your answer an hour from now, or a year from now, it's not at your core. We often look back on our childhood to understand the deep-seated dreams we have for our children. Unfulfilled dreams can often be projected onto our children as unwelcome expectations. It's a good idea to check and own such reflective expectations rather than burdening our offspring with them. Projected expectations can cause years of hurt and disappointment for both the parent and the child, straining the relationship.

Looking Back to Move Forward

Dreams almost always have a backstory. Your WHY may be hiding behind an experience that left you feeling great joy, immense pain, or a sense of wonder. At the root of WHY, there is freedom, joy, and peace. There is also the opportunity to accomplish great things, build your empire, or turn your life around completely.

For Janet, she grew up actively involved in charity work. Her parents took her to the soup kitchen on weekends and holidays. She volunteered at an animal shelter during college and found great pride in ringing the little red bell outside a department store around Christmastime. Her current position was so time-consuming she barely had the energy to cook dinner for herself, let alone look after anyone or anything else. While she was on vacation in Florida, a hurricane hit. Rather than cancel the rest of her vacation, she stayed for five days after the hurricane and helped with cleanup efforts. She cried with those who had lost everything and rejoiced with the families who were reunited after the storm.

Janet's experience reminded her that there was life outside the four walls of her office and her uptown apartment. When examining her own WHY, she found that helping others was at the root of who she was and was ingrained in her from a young age. She decided that something in her life had to change. She either had to work fewer hours, or she had to change to a position that allowed her to live within her purpose. She made a plan that looked something like this:

1. Discuss a four-day workweek with my boss.

2. If a four-day workweek is a no-go, begin researching a new position that is in the nonprofit sector or that would allow for a shorter workweek.

3. Identify local nonprofits to share my time and talents with in a meaningful way.

Within six months, Janet was working a four-day workweek at her current company. She spent her Fridays working at a battered women's shelter, helping victims learn how to manage money as they started their new life outside of abusive relationships. Since she stayed at her current company, she kept her high salary, which also allowed her to make financial donations to the shelter. As a bonus, her company also came on board as a sponsor for the shelter's yearly fundraiser. Janet was happier than she had been in years. She found her purpose, developed a plan, and believed she could do it.

It's easy to get comfortable in life, and comfortable may feel good for a while, but eventually, your true self will come knocking, asking for some much-needed attention.

When you're in search of what your WHY should look like, go through these writing exercises:

1. When was a time that I felt complete joy? Where was I, what was I doing, who was there? How did I feel? Is there a way to replicate this feeling?

_____

_____

_____

_____

2. What are some of my favorite childhood memories? Why did these stick with me?

_____

_____

_____

_____

3. What am I currently doing or want to be doing that would make my children (or future children) proud that I am their parent?

_____

_____

_____

_____

Not all WHYs come from some rainbow and a buttery childhood dream. Some come from dark places, fear, bad experiences, and that small voice that says, "You deserve better." If that's your story, know that you are not alone. Also know that some of the strongest, most determined WHYs come from the desire not to be or do something. Knowing what you don't want to do or become is a legitimate part of the success equation. The world often spends too much time dictating what success looks like and not enough time helping people break out of negative narratives.

There is still more to Janet's WHY story. When she went to volunteer her time at the shelter for battered women, she befriended the owner, Tracie, who was very passionate about the work she was doing. Tracie told her that she was once a highly successful lawyer, but after missing an important trial due to a violent beating by her spouse, she knew things had to change. To the world, Jack, Tracie's husband, was the dream husband and a great provider, but he was a monster to Tracie. What started as verbal insults turned to physical violence and extreme emotional abuse. To the world, Tracie was a high-powered, no-nonsense attorney, but inside, she was crumbling.

Like many people in her situation, Tracie was ashamed, embarrassed, and so beat down, she didn't think there was a way out. She often blamed herself for Jack's actions and her own stupidity for marrying him. What changed? After years of well-meaning friends telling her she should leave, one asked her to look at her life and dream a new dream, to find her WHY. Did being an attorney married to a physically abusive spouse serve some greater purpose in her life, or was she stuck in her situation due to fear, doubt, and myriad other emotions? Tracie's friend gave her a journal and asked her to write a letter to her eight-year-old self, asking that eight-year-old self if she was living in her purpose and making her proud. Had she become the woman her eight-year-old self knew she could be?

After many tear stained pages, Tracie found the courage to make a change. She had a WHY that was so powerful she began winning case after case and stashing her winnings. After a year, Tracie left, got a divorce, and used her painful experiences from her failed marriage to help others get out of similar situations. She realized that her law degree wasn't a waste; it was perfect for helping her start a 501(c)(3) and manage the ins and outs of running it. She was also the person these women could trust to sort out their messy legal matters once they left their own abusive situations because she had been there and done that.

At the core of who Tracie was, there was this eight-year-old girl who loved to solve problems. She was always the one in the group of friends that people could count on, and she was incredibly intelligent. She made a plan to turn her life around. That plan had actionable items and a timeline. She also believed that she could do it. Tracie was using the WHY method without having ever read this book.

The WHY method isn't rocket science. It isn't some secret or complicated scientific method. It follows common sense and human nature. We can all find our WHY if we dig deep, look carefully at the good and bad memories that shape who we are at our core, have a desire to live in our purpose, and believe we can do it.